D1442085

a treasury of NEEDLECRAFT GIFTS for the NEW BABY

a treasury of
NEEDLECRAFT GIFTS
for the NEW BABY

JEAN RAY LAURY

Taplinger Publishing Company / New York

First Edition

Published in the United States in 1976 by
TAPLINGER PUBLISHING CO., INC.,
New York, New York

Published simultaneously in the Dominion of Canada by
Burns & MacEachern, Ltd., Ontario

Library of Congress Cataloging in Publication Data

Laury, Jean Ray
    A treasury of needlecraft gifts for the new baby.

    1. Needlework. 2. Infants' supplies. I. Title.
TT751.L38   1976   746.4   76-12186

ISBN 0-8008-7858-2

Photographic Credits

By Gayle Smalley: Pages 2–3, 14, 15, 16, 20, 21, 23, 27, 29, 35, 36, 37,
40R, 41, 43, 45, 50, 52, 59, 61, 62, 63, 64, 65, 76, 77, 78, 79, 83, 84, 90, 96,
98, 99, 111L, 116, 120–121, 127, 128, 132, 135, 137, 160, 161, 167,
168, 169, 170, 172, 173, 174, and 189.

By Stan Bitters: Pages 9, 10, 17, 18, 19, 24, 26, 31, 34, 38, 40L, 42, 44,
47, 48, 53, 54, 55, 56, 57, 66, 68–69, 72, 73, 74, 75, 86, 88, 89, 94, 100,
105, 109, 111R, 112, 115, 117, 119, 121, 123, 125, 129, 130–131,
138, 140, 141, 144, 146, 147, 149, 151, 154, 155, 156, 158, 159, 162, 163,
165, 171, 174, 179, and 187.

By Gene Spurlock: Page 102.

All work in this book is by the author, except where another
designer is credited.
All drawings and illustrations are the work of the author.

The title spread illustration is from Lynette Hiebert's work,
"Tree with a Hammock."

Designed by Mollie M. Torras

acknowledgments

Many artists generously lent their work for this book; my warmest thanks to Shirli Adkins, Bets Barnard, Priscilla Beeching, Wilanna Bristow, Christine Cavanaugh Davenport, Tyna and Wayne Donelson, Betty Ferguson, Bonnie Floyd, Melanie Fogle, Lynette Hiebert, Doris Hoover, Karen Jahncke, Pat King, Mog Miller, Betsy Mitchell, Olga Seeley, Ernie Smith, Diana Van Wagoner Speer, Nina Stull, Nancy Taylor, Nancy Welch, Brian Wilhite, and Carol Zellmer.

Two beautiful models posed patiently (if unknowingly)—to Quinn Gomez-Heitzeberg and Chelsea Wilhite and their mothers, my thanks.

I am also grateful to The Wicker Carriage in Fresno, California, for the loan of the carousel horse and the Victorian wicker furniture, and to Rosalie Balakian for her cradle.

Special words of appreciation to my husband, Stan Bitters, and to Gayle Smalley for their superb photography.

contents

9. *Methods*   177

illustrations in color

9

about gifts for babies

The arrival of a new baby is an event to be celebrated! This book offers a bright, colorful collection of ideas to make the celebration more beautiful.

The joy over the birth of a child is a universal one. Birth offers a sense of personal history—the mother completes a link between the grandparent and grandchild. Both father and mother see the newborn as an extension of their own life-forces. Grandparents view a continuation of names (either first or last) as a link in the same way that brown eyes or curly hair may be inherited by one generation from the last. Both excitement and sentiment accompany the anticipated arrival.

According to legend, someone once asked Benjamin Franklin (as he strung a key onto his kite string), "What good is electricity?" He supposedly answered by asking, "What good is a baby?", thus reminding us all of the potential in anything new—and particularly in human life. Our joy comes partly, then, in recognizing the unique potential of each baby born to someone we love.

There is a special delight in using baby things that have been treasured and passed from parent to child. How exquisite the quilts and how beloved the teddy bears or bibs that have survived for three generations!

These curly-headed dolls are made of
stuffed cotton socks. By Karen Jahncke.

Fabric acrobat clings to his trapeze with Velcro hands.

If only a few rare articles have survived in your own family, this seems a
perfect time to start a new cycle. A distinctive gift will be thoroughly enjoyed and then folded in tissue and boxed for the next child or the next
generation. When it is later unwrapped, what comes out of the box is many
times greater than the fabric and ribbon of which it is made—out come
nostalgic recollections and family remembrances.

This book offers a treasury of gift ideas, mostly needlework, which
you can make for the baby. Some, such as bibs and blankets, meet prac-

tical, everyday needs. Others have a ceremonial import—like christening gowns or name panels. Still others are for older brothers or sisters, to help them share in the joy of a new baby. Siblings are not always ecstatic about the newcomer, so here are toys to remind them that they, too, are still special. There are gifts for parents, for the baby's room, and for going out.

Some gifts are richly traditional while others are fresh and original. What is probably most significant with any of these gifts is that they are handmade and personal. There is as much joy and pleasure in making them as there is in receiving and using them. So be sure, when you finish a quilt for the new baby, to embroider the baby's name and birth date on the border. Then add your own name, because special presents have a way of surviving.

A baby enjoys a comfortable padded patchwork nap pad with a pillow.

I. *vital statistics*

Names and birth dates take on a special significance for the parents of a newborn. A panel to commemorate the particular date may be made in any of several ways, depending on your own skills and talents. If you are already adept with needlepoint or crewel stitchery, take advantage of your talents and incorporate those in your work. Or use the birth announcement sent in the mail and elaborate on it. Handprints or footprints are nice additions when they are available, as are photographs.

The designs shown here can be produced in a variety of ways. An appliqué panel could be translated to paint, if you feel more at home with a brush than a needle. A needlepoint design can be executed in embroidery. Adapt any of the ideas shown to your favorite ways of working and you'll enjoy the project more and probably have greater success.

Felt Name Panel

Chelsea's name and birth date are recorded in the clear bright colors of felt appliqué. Felt is especially suitable for name panels since the cut edges of felt do not need to be turned under for sewing. Lettering, therefore, can easily be sewn in felt, while it is difficult to sew in most woven fabrics.

13

Chelsea's panel is hand-sewn of felt, then mounted on a plywood panel.

Designs for felt name panel.
(1 square = ½ inch)

The length of the name or month to be appliquéd will determine the size of the felt shape behind it. If necessary, letters can be made smaller to fit them into the space. For directions on cutting lettering, see page 188.

This panel was finished at thirteen inches by sixteen inches, but be sure to cut the felt 2 or 3 inches larger at each edge if you plan to mount the background piece of felt over plywood. A rectangle about 18 inches by 21 inches will be adequate. You will also need a ½-inch (13-mm) plywood board cut to the size of the finished panel. Chelsea's panel was mounted. The felt could also be hemmed and hung from a rod if that is preferred.

Pattern pieces for the leaves, circles, heart, and flowers are on the grid. The heart may be cut from felt, or (as it is here) from wood. A roofing shingle provided the wood, though any wood ¼ of an inch (6 mm) thick will do. Leave the wood natural or stain lightly.

Arrange the lettering, then sew it in place using a single strand of embroidery floss. Here, yellow felt letters are sewn to green. A whipstitch or tiny overcast stitch is easy to do. After sewing the lettering, cut out the green shape and sew it onto a white felt backing piece. Then cut again, around the entire shape, and sew the white to a background of yellow felt. Finally, add the decorative leaves, dots, and flowers.

To finish the panel, either by mounting or hemming, see the directions on pages 184 and 185. The name panel makes a delightful gift for the new baby, the nursery, or the beaming parents.

David's Panel

An even simpler name panel can be made by applying lettering directly to a background panel of felt. This simplifies the cutting as well as the sewing.

The background felt is cut 16 inches (41 cm) wide and 18 inches (46 cm) long. Lettering for the name and date is cut according to the section on lettering on page 188. Measure from the top or bottom to assure even lines of lettering. The heart pattern is the same as the one for Chelsea's panel, as are the dots and flowers. The birds, from the drawing on the grid, are cut and sewn in place with a whipstitch.

Felt, hung over a rod, provides the backing for David's whipstitched name panel.

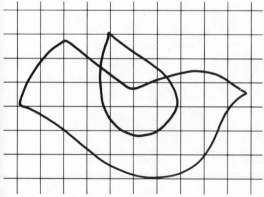

Bird for David's panel. (1 square = ½ inch)

David's panel was hung from a rod, so there is a channel at the top to hold the rod. Use either a wide ribbon or a strip of felt cut the width of the panel and about 2 inches deep. Sew it to the top edge of the panel with a running stitch, leaving the ends open. Use a wood dowel or a brass curtain rod in the channel.

Lettering Set Panel

For those who are reluctant to tackle lettering, an easy solution is to use a child's printing set (the kind that has rubber or composition letters). It avoids the problem of handcut lettering entirely.

By doing the lettering on a separate sheet of fabric, you can easily discard any errors. Print the name and date and when they are finished, cut around them to make rectangles. The ones shown here are 4¼ inches by 5½ inches for the date and 3¼ inches by 8½ inches for the name. Remember that these measurements fit this name. If you print a longer name, you will want to alter the size of the rectangle. An additional allowance must be made at the edges so that the material can be hemmed and whipstitched to the rectangles of felt. The felt pieces that outline the lettering are cut ½ of an inch (13 mm) larger than the finished size of the printed cloth. The

Anne's panel is printed with India ink and a child's printing set, then appliquéd.

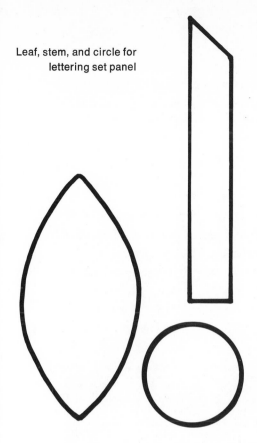

designs for the leaves, circles, and stems are given full size.

In this panel the background felt was cut 15 inches wide by 20 inches long. When the lettering has been appliquéd to the background, the leaves, stems, and circles are added. Each is whipstitched using a single strand of sewing thread in a matching color. To form a channel at the top edge for hanging, sew on a strip of felt the width of the panel and about 2 inches deep. Use a running stitch and sew it as described for David's panel.

The printing set makes possible the use of more extensive lettering. The place of birth, weight at birth, and parents' names can easily be included. The printing set may be a valuable aid if you plan to appliqué a family tree, where lettering requirements are even greater.

Plaid Footprint Panel

Michael's mother traced around his foot to get the pattern for this simple but delightful appliqué. The footprint was cut from a plaid fabric

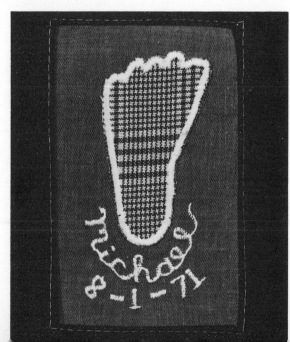

Michael's footprint panel is machine-appliquéd on blue cotton, then framed with a heavy denim border. By Nina Stull.

17

and machine-appliquéd with satin stitch onto a pale blue cotton. The name and date are also machine-embroidered using a satin stitch. The finished appliqué was framed in dark blue denim, and machine-stitched at the edge. On the back, a small plastic ring provides a device for hanging.

Christopher's Footprint Panel

For anyone already adept in needlepoint, footprints may provide the inspiration for a panel similar to Christopher's. The prints are first placed centrally on the canvas and drawn in with needlepoint markers. Then the remaining pattern and lettering must be worked out according to the methods used in this technique. Karen Jahncke, who designed and made this panel for her son, included his weight and birth date. She added a border design to frame the needlepoint and repeated the colors of the lettering. Many needlepoint books give specific directions for lettering.

Needlepoint was used by Karen Jahncke for her son Christopher's footprint panel.

Embroidered Name Panel

Noah's ark provided the theme for this exquisitely sewn name panel. Christine Cavanagh Davenport designed the panel, which was stitched with

This beautiful embroidered name panel was designed by Christine Cavanagh Davenport to proclaim her son's birth. Her sister, Kasey Cavanagh, stitched it with cotton embroidery floss on linen.

embroidery floss on linen, for her son. The pertinent information was tucked in between the animals and the ark. Any similar drawing or illustration can be adapted to embroidery in the same way. The design must first be drawn or traced onto tracing paper. Then embroidery transfer pencils (available in needlework shops) are used to transfer the design to fabric. Two strands of embroidery floss were used in satin stitch, chain stitch, French knots, buttonhole, and herringbone stitches.

A sunshiny welcome
for the new baby, designed by
Nina Stull.

Welcome Panel

A combination of hand sewing and machine sewing was used for this charming panel made to welcome the new baby. A 6-inch (15-cm) circle provides the base onto which the fabric shapes are sewn to suggest a landscape. As the pieces are hand-appliquéd, they are also padded. The "Welcome" is machine-sewn through the fabric and stuffing, while the details at the top are hand-embroidered. A line of piping or cording was added at the outside edge to finish the circle. Additional stuffing helps make the disk somewhat stiff.

The pattern for the petals or sun rays is on the grid. Add a seam allowance. They are sewn, right sides facing, except for the top, then turned right side out. Stuffing and quilting make them somewhat rigid, so that they hold their shapes. The petals are pinned in place, then slip-stitched to the

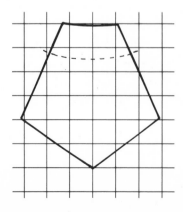

Petals or sun rays for the welcome panel. The dotted line indicates the part beneath the central circle. (1 square = ½ inch)

back. A circle of felt, cut 5½ inches (14 cm) in diameter, is stitched onto the back to cover the open edges of the petals. A small plastic ring is stitched to the top back to serve as a hanger.

Add your own variations and touches to a personal welcome. A sun, a flower, or a moon—all offer decorative areas for quilting and stitching.

Pennants

The neighborhood is awaiting news! Have a panel or flag ready to hang to announce the latest arrival. It can be prepared up to the point of adding "Boy" or "Girl"—or do one panel of each and be completely prepared.

These banners can be presented to the parents a week or two before the due date and then either can be hung out as soon as the vital statistics are available.

A neighborhood will enjoy sharing a banner to be passed from one house to another, as needed, to herald new arrivals.

The gingerbread figures in the first two panels are cut from cotton

Fabric adhesive provides a speedy method of appliqué for news-bearing pennants.

Gingerbread figures for pennants. (1 square = ½ inch)

fabric. They are bonded to the background with a two-faced adhesive fabric. Stitch Witchery is the brand name of one such double bonding material. The gingerbread girls in the third panel are cut from felt and bonded in the same way.

The patterns for the figures are on the grid. Three-inch-high (8-cm) lettering of printed cotton, gingham, or felt is cut according to directions

Heart pattern for the small "It's a girl" pennant

Rubber-stamp lettering was used to print these small pennants, just five inches wide and nineteen inches long.

on page 188. These particular pennants measured ten inches by forty-six inches.

On the small pennants with the hearts, the lettering is printed with a rubber-stamp lettering set. The large heart is identical to the one on page 14. The smaller heart is full size in the drawing.

Along with those gifts that celebrate the birth date are those that celebrate other special occasions. The naming of the baby is certainly one! The ceremonial importance of the event varies among different religions, but in almost all, the occasion calls for special pillows, wraps, or clothes. Christenings and baptisms are among those rituals for which special articles are often made. A first trip to visit grandparents is an occasion requiring festive or special wear. And family observances of any kind call for distinctive attire.

A marvelous way to personalize a christening quilt is to incorporate old family needlework into the design. Here are two quilts which make special use of crochet and needle-lace forms.

Pink Christening Quilt

A single, special crochet doily was used medallion-like for the center of this luscious velveteen quilt. It provides a lovely way of incorporating

A pink-edged doily forms the central motif of this luxurious christening quilt.

the handwork of a grandmother or great-grandmother. Certainly the sentiment and nostalgia add another dimension to the use of the quilt.

A square of white velveteen was used at the center. It was cut large enough to accommodate the doily with several inches to spare. This doily was a large one, edged in pink, and destined to remain in a drawer for the rest of its natural life—until it was launched on a new career as quilt top.

The doily was placed on a square of white velveteen. Before the doily was sewn in place, a circle of pink velveteen was appliquéd exactly in the center. Then, when the crochet was placed on top, the white pattern showed clearly over the pink. The remainder of the doily created a white-on-white pattern outlined in bright pink. The doily was held securely in place with several rows of tacking stitches.

Bands of velveteen were then added to the white square, going from light pink to dark pink, then to red and finally wine. The outside edge was bound in dark pink. The sizes of the bands can be made larger or smaller, depending on the desired finished size. Obviously the size of the needlework or doily will also affect the final dimensions. The bands on this quilt, starting next to the white, are 3 inches, 5 inches, 3 inches, and 2 inches. These are finished sizes, so seam allowance must be added. The binding is 1½ inches (38 mm) wide, but since it wraps around the raw edge of the quilt another 1½ inches (38 mm) must be allowed for the back, plus the seam.

The finished quilt is approximately fifty inches square. This is ample for wrapping and carrying the baby or as a crib or carriage cover.

The quilt was assembled with batting as described on page 179. It is quilted with machine sewing which follows the seam lines of each band as well as the edge of the doily. Some hand tacking was required at the center of the doily to hold it flat.

Blue Christening Quilt

The blue quilt displays an individual collection of needlework. This provides a way of including heirloom pieces from godparents, from friends, or from both families.

A single piece of cotton velveteen fabric, cut approximately 37 inches by 45 inches provided the base for this quilt. The needlework and handmade edging are placed in a symmetrical arrangement, then tacked in place. When you sew, use a strong white thread and tiny stitches. A bright

This christening quilt uses pieces of lace belonging to the baby's family.

green backing was selected and, in this case, a blanket provided the filler. It is hand-quilted according to the directions on page 181. The quilting stitches echo the shapes of the lacework. Binding is made of the same blue.

Baptismal Pillow

This sparkling delicate pillow is obviously meant to be used for selected occasions such as christenings or baptisms. It would be impractical
for everyday use and probably not comfortable for a baby's cheek to rest
against for an extended time. However, it provides a fittingly elegant head-
rest for a significant event of any kind.

The basic pillow may be a purchased ready-made one, or it may be
made of fabric-covered Dacron batting. The pillow need not be large, and

A special pillow, used for baptisms or christenings.

this one was a little over twelve inches long. A white pillow cover should be made for the pillow form.

Any special piece of needlework will provide a fitting top. This one, of Irish crochet, is square but a round, rectangular, or oval one will be just as appropriate. Several different pastels of fabric were appliquéd to the pillow cover. These colored areas should be cut to emphasize or exaggerate the designs within the lacework. Here the colored fabrics were cut square to repeat the crochet pattern. Knitted lace, rescued from a pair of antique pillowcases, was added at each edge.

A special pillow of this kind makes a lovely family gift—one which can perhaps be shared by several babies. Made by a grandmother, it could belong equally to all the grandchildren whose names and birth dates could be embroidered on the back.

Zip-up

Another bit of information that *always* needs recording is the growth of the young child. In the zip-up shown here, two sections of felt were joined by the zipper in the middle.

Each side panel is 4½ inches by 28 inches (11 cm by 71 cm), and is backed with a second identical piece of felt. They are machine-sewn together with a line of top stitching. Lettering is machine-stitched to one of the felt panels. See page 188 for directions on cutting lettering.

A part of a colored plastic tape measure is stitched to the second side of the panel. This one starts at 24 inches. When the zipper is opened, there is a panel of white cloth, 6 inches by 21 inches (15 cm by 53 cm) in size. It is slip-stitched to the reverse side so that when the zipper is opened, it reveals the white fabric.

In hanging the growth panel, it is essential that the 24-inch mark on the tape be placed exactly 24 inches above the floor level. Then when a child is measured, his or her height and age can be recorded on the white lining fabric.

This section on vital statistics would not be complete without a family tree. There are many ways of recording the family names, and here is one suggestion:

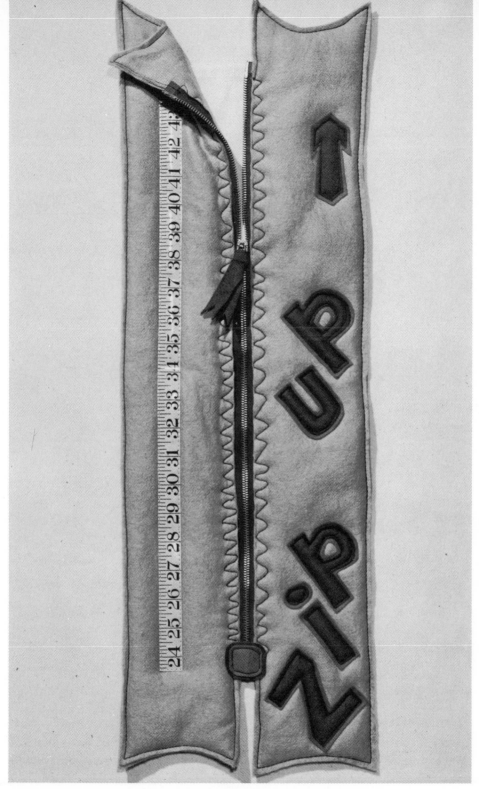

Zip-up panel has white fabric on the inside where children's heights are recorded. By Nina Stull.

Design for appliqué family tree. (1 square = 1 inch)

The leaf pattern

Appliqué Family Tree

This family tree design can be adapted to almost any technique. The shapes used in the felt appliqué of the panel are in the drawings on the grid. The leaf is a full-size pattern. The same shapes can be used for embroidery or needlepoint. To use the design for appliqué, just add a seam allowance to each edge.

The lettering for this family tree can be added in any of several ways. Perhaps the most attractive (and the most time-consuming) is embroidery. Permanent marking pen can be used on some fabrics. It is safer to write on a fabric tape and then to sew the tape onto the appropriate space. This approach is also best on felt. Children's printing sets may be used on fabric

Appliqué family tree, fifteen inches wide.

and then the printed names can be appliquéd to the tree. These methods avoid the possibility of spoiling the panel with a misspelled name or a bit of smeared ink.

Finally, there are special colored markers for use on fabric. They are washable and offer a bright array of colors. Vogart and Liquid Embroidery both have pointed tips which make it possible to keep the lettering small. Some practice on scrap fabrics would be advisable before writing directly on your panel.

The tree design can be varied to accommodate as many names as needed. Baby's name and birth date can appear on tree trunk, the parents on the two large branches, grandparents on the next four. All other names can be added to the leaves.

Few gifts will bring more lasting delight than the recording of names and dates on a family tree. Another arrangement for a family tree is shown below.

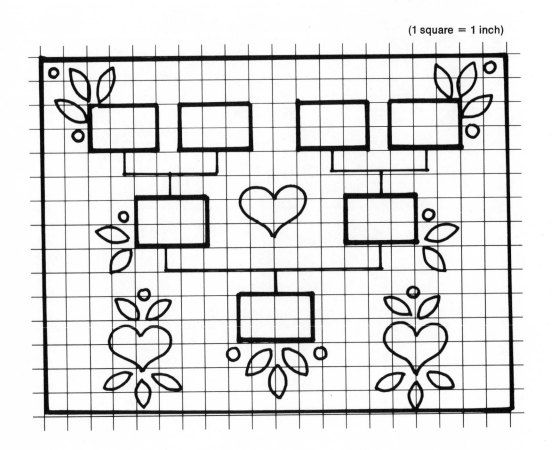

(1 square = 1 inch)

This panel proclaims the birth date in colorful felt appliqué. (Photo by Gayle Smalley)

An exquisitely embroidered name panel, with Noah's ark and a retinue of animals, announces James' birth date. By Christine Cavanagh Davenport. (Photo by Stan Bitters)

Christening quilt combines family needle laces and doilies on a blue velveteen background. (Photo by Stan Bitters)

Machine appliqué designs
brighten a white bib.
(Photo by Stan Bitters)

A baby needs a generous supply of absorbent bibs,
like these made from hand towels.
(Photo by Gayle Smalley)

Racing stripes add a sporting touch to
flannel gowns. (Photo by Gayle Smalley)

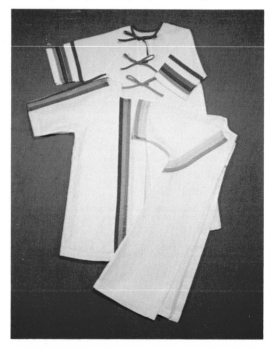

2. gifts for the baby to wear

Most baby clothes are of simple design, since simple cuts allow for maximum comfort. This usually means they can be sewn with ease, and the simplicity of pattern allows for the addition of decorative detail. Many ready-made clothes are ideal for embroidered embellishments or appliquéd details.

Few things are used more consistently over a long period of time than bibs. Tiny babies and toddlers alike have a constant need of them. Following are several varieties of bibs.

All bibs should be made with certain basic considerations in mind. One is that the purpose of the bib is to keep spilled food separated from the baby and/or his clothes. This may be accomplished by lining the bib with flexible plastic or waterproof material or by using a flannel-surfaced rubberized pad for lining. If toweling is used, it will provide ample absorbency. Quilted materials are also thick enough to soak up spilled foods.

A reversible bib will require fabric on each side with plastic or absorbent material sandwiched between. Place the three layers together and pin around the outside edge. Then mark the exact outline on the top fabric and machine-stitch on that line through all three layers. Trim excess material close to the seam and bind with bias tape or other binding.

Rainbow Bib

A large washcloth provides a prefinished bib in an absorbent terry cloth. Cut a half circle from one side, bind with bias tape, and the essentials are complete.

The easily cut cloud shapes are machine-appliquéd to the bib with a wide satin stitch. Bias tape in several colors is machine-zigzagged to form the rainbow.

Rainbow bib is machine-appliquéd on a terry washcloth.

Hand towels convert readily to
absorbent bibs.

Hand Towel Bib

Like the rainbow bib, these sprightly bird bibs are made from pre-finished terry cloth. Two hand towels are needed in each of the two colors. A neck hole is cut in one towel, and bound with bias tape. The second color is used for the appliqué design. That leaves enough terry cloth left over for the blotting pad that is invariably needed for an enthusiastic young spoon handler.

The birds on these bibs are machine-satin-stitched to the terry towel. The pattern is given on the grid. If you decide to hand-appliqué instead, be

Bird motif for hand towel bib.
(1 square = ½ inch)

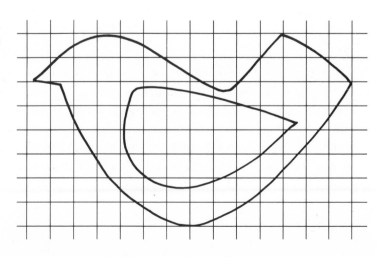

36 sure to allow an additional ¼ of an inch (6 mm) to turn under. For a really robust and energetic toddler, a full-size-towel bib would be welcomed by any mother.

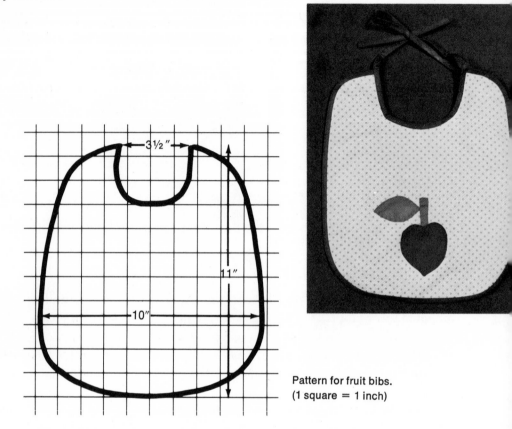

Pattern for fruit bibs.
(1 square = 1 inch)

Fruit Bibs

Three attractive, simple bibs are made from polka-dot fabrics. The appliqué patterns are shown on the grids. Cut according to the pattern for machine appliqué. If you are sewing by hand, as these were sewn, add a seam allowance at each edge. Hand-sew with a running stitch or machine-sew with a satin stitch. The pear seeds are outlined with a simple running stitch.

When the decorative work is complete, line with plastic or flannel and bind with bias tape. First bind the outer edge of the bib. Bind the neck area last, letting tape extend at each end for ties.

Fruit designs, appliquéd to polka-dot
fabrics, make colorful bibs.

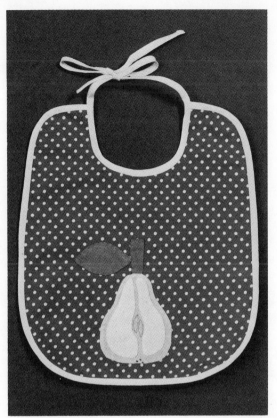

Fruit bib motifs. (1 square = ½ inch)

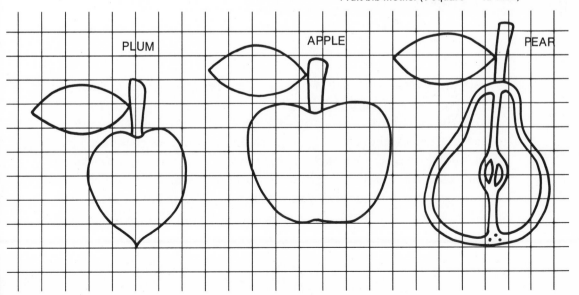

PLUM

APPLE

PEAR

Flower bib has a catchall pocket.

Flower Bib

A simple cotton bib, lined in plastic, has a catchall pocket at the bottom. The pattern is given on the grid. The decorative design is drawn directly on the bib fabric with a permanent fabric marker. Liquid Embroidery and Vogart are two commonly available brands of these markers suitable for use on cloth. See page 186 for further information on markers.

Older children would enjoy participating in bib-making by drawing their own designs on the fabric, either before the bib is cut or after it is assembled. Names and dates may be added to personalize the bib or to celebrate a first birthday.

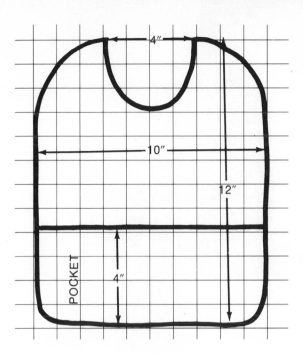

Bird Bib

This detail is another example of the use of ball-point markers for fabric bibs. The Early American design was drawn directly onto the cut bib material before it was lined and bound with bias tape. The photograph shows the textural pattern possible with these ball-point markers.

Ball-point fabric markers add color to a bib. They can be used to color areas solid or to give a crayon-like texture.

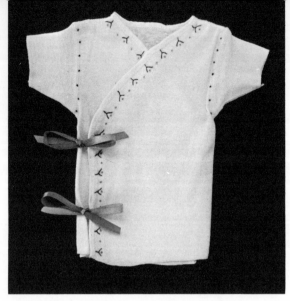

A bright red heart and rows of fly stitches make this shirt special.

Blue and green French knots and flowers add a pretty touch to an ordinary cotton knit shirt.

Baby Shirts

Ready-made cotton shirts for babies are both durable and well sewn. It is easier to buy them and add your own decorative touches. Because the shirts are stretchy, it is difficult to appliqué over the material. Embroidery is more suitable. If batik or tie-dye is among your specialties, either will add elegance to these ordinary little shirts.

One of these shirts has delicate embroidery next to the seam. It consists of a Y stitch (or fly stitch) sewn at right angles to the edge, alternated with French knots. Any similar embroidery stitch can be used. Feather-stitch and double feather are often used on baby clothes. They are flexible stitches and will survive washing and wear without pulling. The cotton ties of this shirt have been replaced with bias-tape ties.

The shirt with the red heart utilizes the same fly stitch, but here it is stacked so that one stitch touches the next. French knots run parallel. The tiny heart is sewn with an outline stitch and red bias tape is substituted for the white cotton ties.

All the embroidery is done using two strands of cotton embroidery floss. Care must be taken so that the stitches are not drawn up too tightly.

Some ease is needed to allow for the stretching of the material as the shirt is pulled on or off the baby.

Training Pants

Training pants are another article which are best purchased ready-made. But decorating them can be fun. For older children, learning to dress themselves, the appliqué of favorite animals will add to the delight of putting on their clothes. A simple outlining in tape adds a sporty look.

Racing stripes in raucous colors turn ordinary cotton pants into a colorful costume. Make stripes to match shirts or dresses. Bias tapes are sewn in place with whipstitches. Sew any vertical stripes first, leaving ends raw. Then when stripes are added at waist and legs, those raw edges are covered. Overlap ends of tape to finish, or turn ends under.

The sun is appliquéd cotton fabric surrounded by French knots. Keep any appliqué rather full (that is, don't pull it tight) as there should be some give in the material. Double-fold bias tape forms the rainbow.

Appliquéing bias tapes to these training pants is an easy way to add dash. The narrow bias rainbow on the right is accompanied by a full sun.

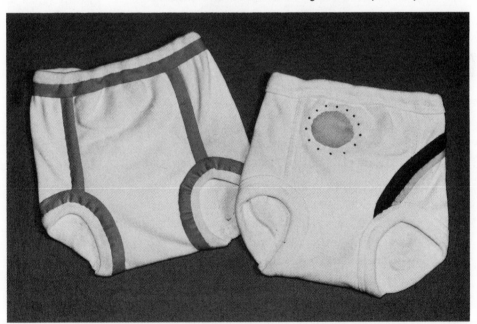

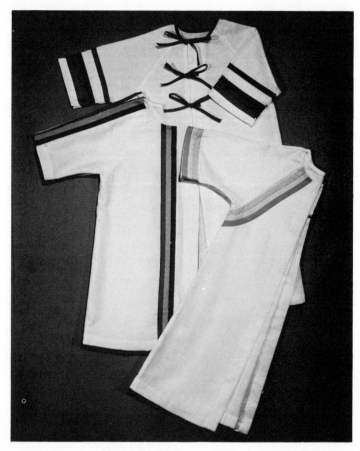

Racing stripes are added to flannel gowns in either
vivid or pastel shades of bias tape.

Flannel Gowns

Ready-made white flannel kimonas or gowns can be perked up with
racing stripes in vivid colors. Versatile folded bias tape offers a quick solution to the problem of making even stripes. On these gowns the stripes
follow construction lines, either in pastels or vibrant combinations. In
sewing the colored tapes, first attach one tape at one side. Then as the
second side is sewn down, catch the first side of the next tape in the same
seam. It will avoid double sewing on any of the lines. A simple whipstitch
or overcast stitch is used. Bias ties are colorful, or Velcro makes an easy
fastener. If you are making the gowns yourself, it is easier to sew the stripes
to the cut flannel pieces before the garment is assembled.

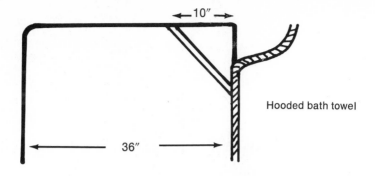

Hooded bath towel

Hooded Bath Towel

Since the bath is an activity enjoyed at least once a day, every baby can easily use an assortment of terry wrap-ups. This lime-green terry-cloth towel is reversed with a flowered fabric print. The hood is formed by securing a triangle of terry cloth (also lined with the print) into one corner. The binding at the outside edge of the towel holds the hood in place.

If 36-inch-wide material is used, the towel can easily be made a yard square. An additional ⅓ of a yard of material is needed for the hood, cut 10 inches long on the right-angle sides. That leaves material for two 12-inch

Terry bath towel, reversed with a bright-patterned fabric, has a corner hood.

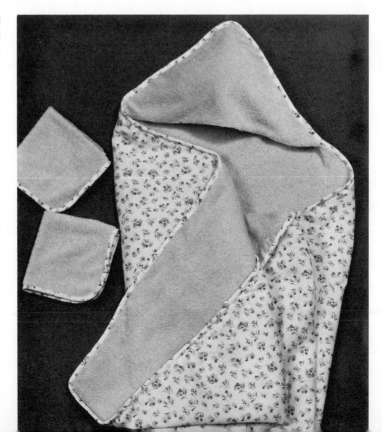

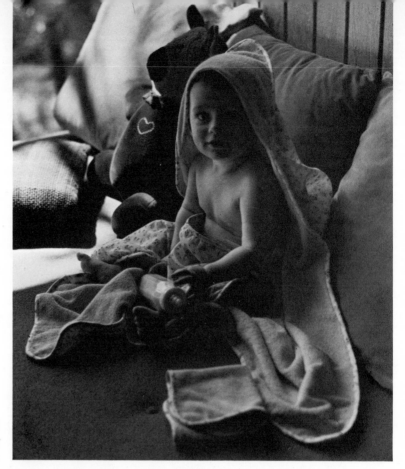

The hooded towel keeps an energetic baby covered after a bath.

washcloths. A yard of 45-inch material provides enough fabric for the towel, a slightly smaller (9-inch) hood, and 9-inch washcloths. Lining material is needed for the towel, the hood, and for the bias binding on the washcloths.

Frog Bath Towel

Another hooded bath wrap-up in terry cloth is made in a different way. A yard of 45-inch terry-cloth toweling is folded diagonally and cut as shown in the drawing. The cut end at the top is stitched across as shown to make a 6-inch (15-cm) seam. Round the corners and finish the raw edge. Leftover material is used for a small washcloth. A machine-appliqué design, as shown in the drawing on the grid, is sewn with satin stitches and wide bias tape finishes the raw edges.

Frog bath towel

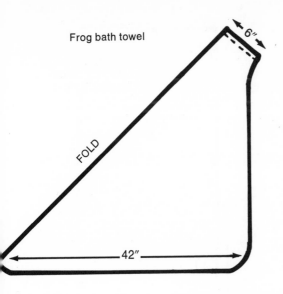

6"

FOLD

42"

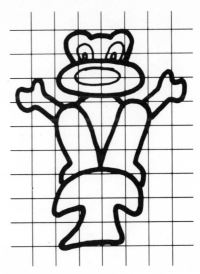

Frog appliqué. (1 square = 1 inch)

Frog bath towel has
a machine-appliqué design.
By Nina Stull.

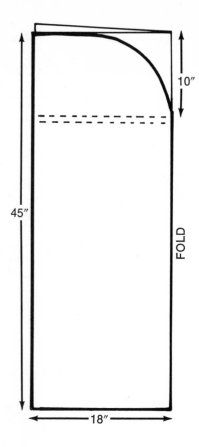

Hooded Robe

A third wrap-up ties at the neck to make a capelike towel. It is most suitable for those babies who can toddle away from the bathtub.

Cut printed fabric for the outside and terry cloth for the inside according to the drawing. Stitch the curved line which forms the hood on both the print and the terry cloth and then, with right sides together and hood seams facing out, join terry cloth to the print from the hem on one side to the hem on the other. Also stitch about three-quarters of the way around the bottom, leaving an opening to turn the fabric right side out. Leave an opening of about 10 inches around 1 inch from the top on each side for the drawstring. Turn fabrics right side out. Sew 2 rows of straight stitching to make a channel for the cord. Run cording through, and secure it at the back to prevent it from pulling out. Hem open area at bottom edge.

Hooded robe ties on and has ample length to wrap up the most active bather.

Bracelets

A perfectly elegant gift in the form of jewelry is shown in these soft, colorful bracelets. Strips of fabric are rolled over, stuffed, and slip-stitched together. Then the ends are overlapped and stitched.

Slip-stitching a bracelet

Try a strip of around 2 inches by 7 inches, then measure it on the wrist of the baby for whom you wish to make the bracelet, since there is considerable variation in sizes. The amount of stuffing used and the stiffness of the fabric also affect the finished size. Remember that a bracelet too

Stuffed fabric bracelets, adorned with embroidery and edgings,
slip easily over the baby's wrist. By Betty Ferguson.

small or too large still makes a marvelous soft toy for the baby to grasp
and wave about in the air.

If you wish, you may make little bags of matching fabric to accompany
the bracelets and to serve as a gift wrap or a storage bag. Drawstrings can
be used to pull the bags shut.

Some bracelets are made of printed flannel or printed cottons. Others
are of chamois, satin, embroidered materials, or solid colors. Rows of edging and laces add to the delicacy and detail. They make charming gifts for
babies to wear as well as safe little playthings which can easily be grasped
by the tiniest of hands.

3. gifts for the baby's room

Any nursery is more fun to decorate when there is a theme or a basic color range with which to work. The subject might be something as simple as a heart which is repeated on pillows, curtains, sheets, and rugs. Or it could be a gaily printed fabric from which appliqués are cut, and from which pillows, sheets, and curtains are made. A soft blue color, a brilliant lime green, or lemon yellow may serve as the unifying theme for the whole room. Rainbow motifs can be treated in almost any color range. Surely the nursery is an area where fantasy and imagination may flower. Fortunately the traditional baby blue and powder pink have given way to the use of radiant sunshiny hues to brighten and cheer the nursery.

Sheets and pillowcases are among the easiest of all articles to appliqué, since they always offer a flat, smooth surface on which to work. Pillows may vary in size, though generally a small flat pillow is considered best for the baby. Standard sizes for pillows and mattresses are listed on page 191. The sizes will vary for a standard baby bed, a bassinet, a basket, or a cradle.

While sheets for bassinets and baskets are smaller, remember, however, that the basket is quickly outgrown. Just one or two small decorative sheets may be sufficient.

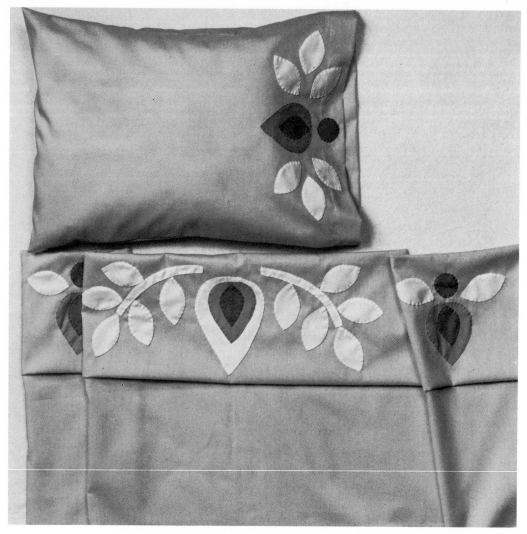

Simple running-stitch hand appliqué is used on this sheet and pillowcase set.

Pink Sheet and Pillowcase

A brilliant pink fabric, appliquéd in white, a deeper pink, and red, adds sparkling color to a baby's room. The material used is part synthetic, so it requires no ironing. But try to select a fabric that is also part cotton for absorbency and comfort.

The finished size of this pillowcase is about thirteen inches by twenty

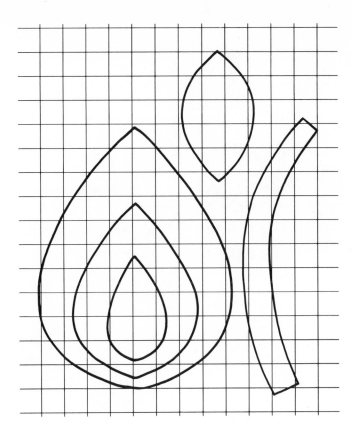

Design for pink sheet appliqué.
(1 square = ½ inch)

inches, which is a little larger than most. Extra fabric on a pillowcase is no problem. It is only if the pillowcase is made too small that it can be a disappointment.

While a fifty-two-inch finished-length sheet is ample for a baby bed, cut extra length for this one if you decide to fold the appliqué section back over the sheet. Since 45-inch material is commonly available, use it full width to take advantage of the two selvages for the sides.

The patterns for the design are on a grid. Add a hem allowance when cutting the shapes, then turn under the edges and sew with a running stitch.

Lace Sheet

The glorious spring green of this sheet and pillowcase is offset by delicate but washable lace edgings. Use antique laces, family heirlooms, or

White edgings and laces add a frosted look to lime green.

Bands of bright blues and greens make a bold design for sheet and pillowcase.

edgings purchased at fabric shops. This set utilizes a combination from the thrift store and the variety store. Machine-sew with straight stitches.

Striped Sheets

This pattern of appliquéd bands is effective on a white backing, but colors can also be used. The bands are cut on the straight of the fabric. Edges are turned under and hemmed by hand, though you can sew them by machine if you prefer. It is easier to sew bands on the pillowcase before seams are joined. The finished sizes of the bands on this set are: green, 1½ inches; blue green, 1 inch; and light blue, 3 inches. Widths can be varied according to preference, and printed fabrics are attractive used with solids. The sheets themselves may be made from bright prints with solid-color bands.

Rainbow Pillows

Rainbows seem to belong to babies! Here is a theme to be carried throughout a room, using the same techniques shown on these pillows.

The set of pillows shown here is sewn with fabric appliqué. The white square for the middle of the pillow is cut first. Then use a plate or a round tray to determine the arc of the rainbow. Cut the first color about 1¼ inches wide and sew the top edge of the curve to the white fabric. Then

Rainbows, appliquéd with many hues to white fabric, make a colorful pillow collection for baby's room.

cut the second color the same width. Overlap the second color on the first, sewing both with one line of stitches. The last colored line will have to be sewn on both edges.

These pillows finish at fourteen inches and a pillow form that is 14 inches (36 cm) or 15 inches (38 cm) will do. You can make your own muslin-covered pillow form (over which to slip the appliquéd pillow cover) or buy a pillow ready-made. Join the pillow top to a pillow back as described on page 185.

It is always advisable to buy (or make) your pillow forms first. Then cut your fabric. If necessary, you can adjust the width of one of the colored bands which outlines the white square to make the pillow top fit a different-size pillow form.

The set of three rainbow pillows shown in the color section is sewn with bias tape. These are much easier to sew, since widths and hems are predetermined. They are less bold in color, but perhaps more baby-like.

Each rainbow is appliquéd onto a square of fabric and outlined with bands of contrasting color. The same rainbow patterns can be used to make curtains, cover a wastebasket, make quilt blocks, or decorate the baby's clothes.

Lace Pillows

Another pattern which can be sprinkled liberally over an entire room is formed by doilies and laces. Here they are combined with red and white fabrics, including tiny polka dots.

A lace doily adds a nostalgic touch to the nursery.

You will want to vary these ideas according to the lacework you have available. The fabrics of the pillow top should be cut and joined first. Then place the doily on top and use tiny tacking stitches to hold it in place. If the crochet is fairly dense, it can be stitched to the pillow top with a line of machine sewing.

These same lace-adorned blocks could be set together for a quilt. Or a row of them could march across the border of a curtain. A red dotted lamp-shade makes an excellent exhibition space for a single circular tatted or crocheted form.

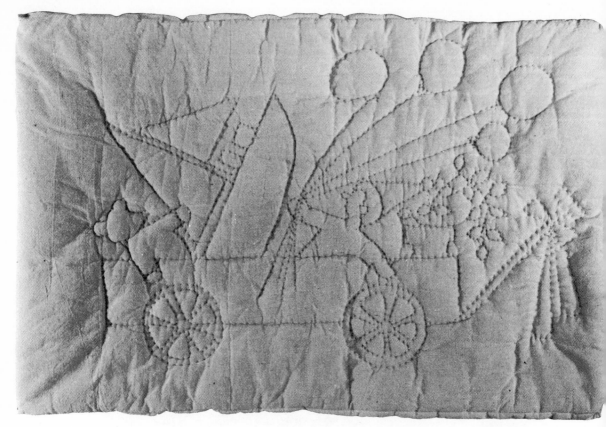

A wagonload of toys rolls across this quilted muslin pillowcase by Priscilla Beeching.

Quilted Pillow

This delightful pillow is padded and quilted muslin. The top of the pillowcase is assembled with backing and filler as for any quilting project (see page 179). Then the drawing is made and transferred to the muslin top. This one was drawn lightly with pencil and washed out after the quilting was finished. Transfer pencils can also be used. When quilting is completed, the top is joined to the pillowcase back and it is hemmed. The finished soft and puffy pillow invites snuggling.

Catchall Bag

This simply made carrier hangs in a car, in the closet, or in the bathroom. Objects of all shapes (powder, lotion, cotton balls, and ointments) can easily be stored or carried in this way. Or use it for dirty clothes or extra clothes while traveling. It is an easy way to keep articles together, and there are no strings or buttons or snaps to be undone.

Select a wooden hanger and saw the ends of the wood off to make it

Catchall bag hangs anywhere and holds anything. Marking-pen drawing is machine-appliquéd to the bag.

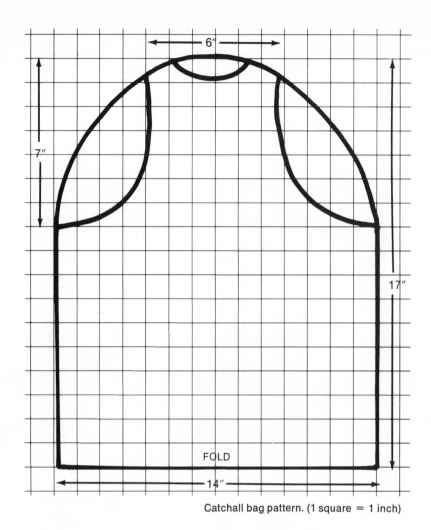

Catchall bag pattern. (1 square = 1 inch)

about 6 inches long. Then cut fabric as shown in the pattern on the grid so that one piece, folded, makes the entire bag. Lining is optional, though a second layer helps give the bag additional body. Any appliqué or embroidery should be added while the parts are still flat. In this one the tree design is done with ball-point fabric markers on white. It is cut out and machine-appliquéd to the bag. Next sew bias binding at top opening and side openings. Then run bias tape from one lower corner in a curve around the raw edges to the other bottom corner. This joins sections and finishes all raw edges.

People Hangers

Wood hangers are needed for these padded, decorated closet luxuries. Saw off the ends so that the hangers are no more than 10 inches to 12 inches across. (If they are too long, they will not fit into a baby's clothing.)

Start with a strip of fabric around 4 inches wide, or wide enough to cover the padding, and leave enough for an overlap. It should be about 2 inches longer than the hanger. Next take synthetic quilt batting or stuffing and glue it to the top edge of the wood hanger. Let it dry. The piece of batting to be glued should be as long as the hanger and wide enough to fold down over each side. Then measure to find the center of the fabric strip. Cut a tiny hole and force the wire hook through this hole. Fold the fabric

With outstretched arms, these people hangers await shirts and dresses.

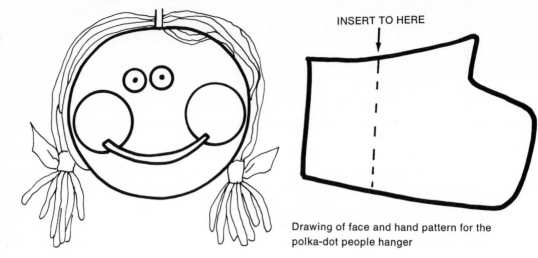

Drawing of face and hand pattern for the polka-dot people hanger

and batting over the hanger, overlapping them at the bottom. Slip-stitch securely at the bottom edge.

To make people hangers, insert felt hands in the ends before stitching them shut. The patterns for the hands are full size. Double thickness will help hold the hands stiff. Either sew or glue the two layers together.

Then slip a fabric powder puff over the wire of the hanger by forcing the wire between the stitches. Don't use too large a powder puff or there will be no room left for the wire hook to fit over a closet pole. When you have determined the placing for the powder puff, slide the puff up and wipe glue onto the wire. Slide puff back down and press, so that the puff is held in place.

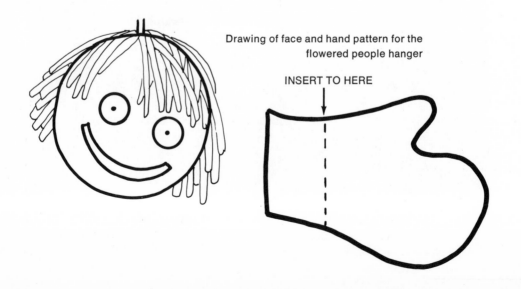

Drawing of face and hand pattern for the flowered people hanger

INSERT TO HERE

Felt features like the ones in the drawings may be appliquéd with an overcast stitch. Cut 12 or more strands of yarn, 10 inches (25 cm) long, for the hair. Tie together in the center. Slip-stitch this knot to the top of the powder puff. Tack down to make pigtails or trim for a short hairdo.

The metal hook of the hanger can be painted with acrylic paint or with enamel. It is best, of course, to paint *before* sewing.

Padded Hangers

For a simple padded hanger, proceed in the same way as in the people hangers. Slip-stitch both the ends and the bottom edge of the fabric.

A length of bias tape can be whipstitched around the metal hook to cover it, or the metal can be painted.

The felt-covered hanger consists of two identical pieces cut by tracing

Hanging up clothes is more pleasant with these padded hangers.

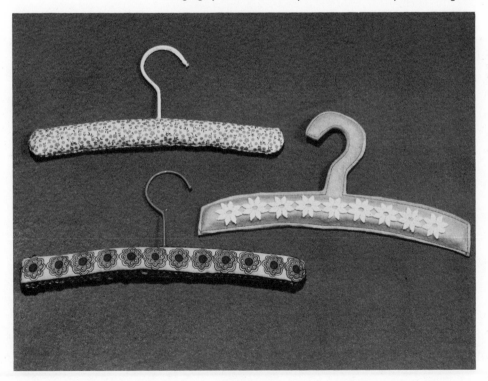

around the hanger. A single line of straight machine stitching holds the felt in place. A lace edging was tacked across the felt-covered hanger to add a decorative detail.

It is a special delight to have padded hangers covered to match dresses. When making other garments, use the remnants to make a matched set.

Lace Panels: Rabbit and Hen

Here is a marvelous way to include grandmother or great-aunt in the nursery. If you have old needle lace, tatting, or crochet, use it in an animal cutout. Remnants and scraps of lace can be used as well as whole pieces.

First cut a background fabric. Either felt or woven material can be used. The ones shown here are 15 inches by 18 inches *plus* the turn-under allowance. Allow around 3 inches to each edge if you plan to pull the background over a plywood board. To make a wall hanging, cut the sides and

Leftover lace remnants are used to collage this delicately detailed rabbit.

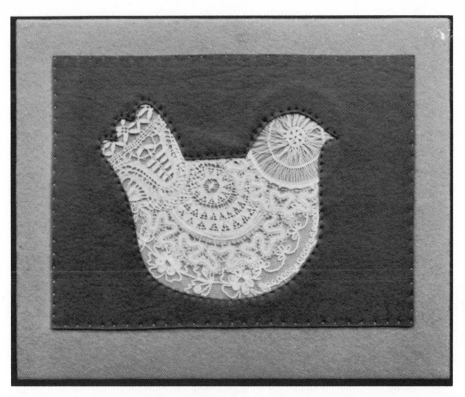

The hen shape has been cut away and the remaining background is used for appliqué over lace. Fifteen inches by eighteen inches.

bottom to the size you wish and add 2 inches (5 cm) at the top edge to fold over. This will make a channel to hold a rod for hanging.

The second piece of material is a somewhat smaller rectangle. The ones used here were 12 inches by 15 inches. It must be felt, and from it cut a simple drawing of an animal. If there is an older child in the family, you can probably get a whole zoo of animals on ten minutes' notice. Be sure to select a simple shape with large open areas. Cut the animal out of the felt, and keep the rectangle from which the animal is cut.

Place the rectangle of felt onto the background panel and pin it at the outside edge. Place laces under the cutout, slipping them under the edge of the cut felt. Overlap raw or torn edges with finished edges of lace. When a pleasing arrangement is made, remove the felt animal cutout and tack the laces in place. Use a thread that matches the color of the lace. Then replace the felt animal and sew both the outside edge of the felt rectangle and the cutout edge of the animal. Use a running stitch or French knots to sew the felt. Then mount or hem.

Stitchery Panels

Small colorful panels are attractive in the baby's room as well as appealing to the beginning stitcher. These are all machine-sewn.

A little collection of black thread drawings of flowers, butterflies, and mythical animals was machine-sewn by Nina Stull on yellow and pink

Tiny stitchery drawings on fabric.
Three inches to four inches wide.

Rainbow pillows in radiant hues are a lively addition to the baby's carriage or room. (Photo by Stan Bitters)

Garden stitchery, for the baby's room, is machine-sewn by designer Nina Stull. (Photo by Gayle Smalley)

Hand-appliquéd sheets and pillowcase made from brilliant pink yardage. (Photo by Gayle Smalley)

The primary colors which are the favorites of children make up this traditional octagonal star pattern quilt. (Photo by Stan Bitters)

A closet carryall bag for toys or extra clothes goes from the closet to car. (Photo by Stan Bitters)

Brother dolls of felt appliqué sport a ball-fringe hairdo. (Photo by Gayle Smalley)

For the budding naturalist in
the nursery, a machine-stitched
spider on checked gingham.
Three inches square.

fabrics. Varying the background of the spider in her web added a new
dimension to the third panel. The fabrics are stretched over wood blocks
and framed.

A garden scene panel has seed packets on sticks making high points
of the design. Fabrics are overlapped and are held in place with lines of
straight machine stitching. Then designs are machine-embroidered over
the tops of the fabrics.

Miniature stitchery panel,
with machine sewing, adds a garden
to the nursery. Six inches square.

Octagonal star quilt, a well-known American patchwork pattern.

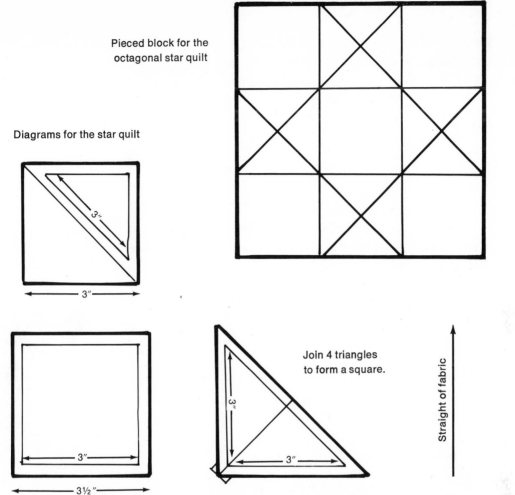

Pieced block for the
octagonal star quilt

Diagrams for the star quilt

3″

3″

3″

3½″

3″

Join 4 triangles
to form a square.

3″

Straight of fabric

Octagonal Star Quilt

No nursery is complete without at least one traditional quilt. This one is for a basket, a bassinet, or cradle since it is small. Additional rows of blocks can be added to reach any desired size.

The pieced blocks are 10½ inches (27 cm) square. They are joined with bands of purple fabric 2½ inches (6.4 cm) wide, making this quilt about three feet by four feet.

Join the pieces into squares according to the drawing. The squares are cut 3½ inches (9 cm) and the squares are halved diagonally to form the triangles. Seam allowance must be made at all cut edges. When the star blocks have been pieced, join two of the star blocks by placing a solid-colored band between them. Then add a third block, so that the three make a strip. Assemble the next strips in the same way. Then join the strips to one another with pieces of solid-colored fabric cut as long as the strips. This makes assembling the quilt easy since no corners are joined.

Directions for quilting and binding are given on pages 181–183.

Nap Pad

Not all naps are taken in bed. When nappers prefer other spots or when babies need a quiet spot to enjoy their milk, here's a comforting nap pad.

Nap pad, colorful
and sturdy, invites the baby to be
"at home" anywhere.

The squares in this pad finish at 5 inches by 5 inches (13 cm by 13 cm).
If you take ½-inch (13-mm) seams, cut the fabric into 6-inch (15-cm) squares.

Join the blocks in rows, then join the rows to one another. For this pad, 5 blocks are used for the width and 8 for the length, making a total of 40 squares. The finished quilt is an ample size for a nap pad.

After the squares are joined to make the quilt top, the quilt is assembled as described on page 179. It is machine-quilted with straight lines of stitching that follow exactly on the seam lines. It is bound according to the directions for binding on page 182, and the binding is stuffed to give a full, rounded, finished edge to the pad.

The matching pillow is made and assembled in the same way. But in the pillow, the finished squares are 4 inches by 4 inches (10 cm by 10 cm)

and 16 are used for the pillow top. After the machine quilting is completed, the pillow top is joined to a backing and sewn as described on page 186.

To make this pad for a playpen, join additional blocks at one side to form a square. (Measure the playpen!) Then add a tie at each corner to secure the pad in position.

4. gifts for siblings

This section regarding the siblings of new babies has two purposes: One is to suggest ways of inviting an older brother or sister to participate in preparations for the baby; the other is to offer ideas for gifts or toys to remind the sibling that he or she, too, is still special!

Children's drawings have a direct appeal and charm which makes them particularly appropriate for use on baby gifts. Drawings made on paper can be transferred to fabric to be worked in appliqué, embroidery, or fabric markers. Here are a few projects in which older brothers and sisters can participate.

"Me in My House" Coverlet

Even a single drawing is ample to provide the design for a quilt or cover. This drawing by a four-year-old shows "me in my house." The drawing was repeated and reversed, then colored in with ball-point markers. The drawings are on white fabric with bands of colored material between them. Because this little cover was small, only 22 inches by 24 inches, it was just backed and not quilted.

If you give the child a piece of paper cut to the size of the finished quilt

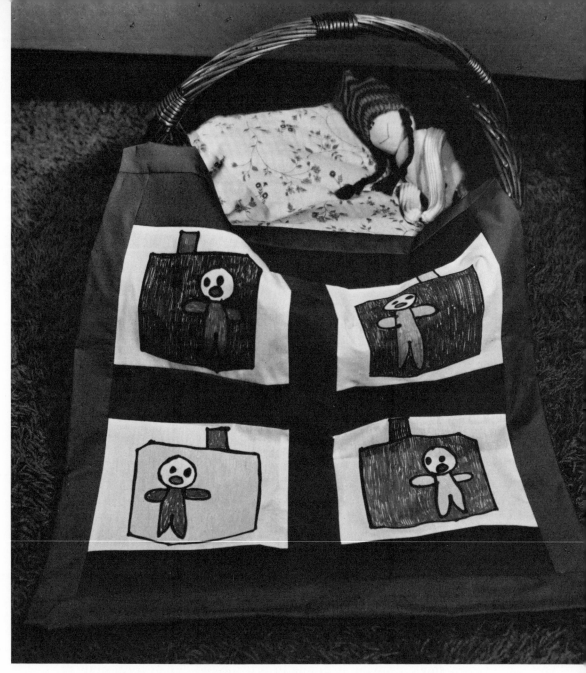

Coverlet made from a preschooler's drawing called "Me in My House."

block, it is easy to insure that the drawing will fit. Obviously, the design can be repeated to make a quilt of whatever size is desired. There are limitless possibilities for making quilts with children's drawings. A collection of drawings gives the most colorful and active pattern, though any number can be used. See page 186 for additional information on the use of various fabric-marking pens.

Mouse Pillow

A small girl's contribution to the baby's room is this mouse pillow. It was drawn with ball-point markers, then cut square and bordered with a bright-colored fabric. Watching the drawing being transformed into a three-dimensional form is an exciting process for any child. Several drawings, each bordered with a different cheerful color, make a pretty addition to the

Mouse pillow is one little girl's idea of what the new baby would enjoy.

baby's room. Many children prefer, naturally, to present the pillow to Mother rather than the new baby! Directions for pillow assembly are given on page 186.

The other drawings photographed would adapt equally well to quilts

Children's drawings
ready to become part of a quilt,
a pillow, or curtains in
the nursery.

or pillows. Drawings with large simple shapes are most easily appliquéd. The finished fabric blocks can be sewn onto carryall bags, toy bags, flannel receiving blankets, or used as pockets on Mother's apron.

Pumpkin Pillows

The pumpkin pillows, made by five- and six-year-olds, suggest a marvelous way for siblings to help get the nursery ready. Obviously, apples, pears, plums, suns, or fish would work as well. If the child selects a complex shape, such as a dog or a horse, just cut an oval or rectangular pillow around the drawing.

Pumpkin pillows,
painted in acrylic on fabric
by children.

Children painted these pumpkins with large brushes, applying acrylic paints directly to the fabric. When the paint was dry, the shapes were cut out and sewn into pillows. Any permanent ink or dye can be used, but be sure to read labels and regard any precautions on the handling of dyes and paints. Many fabric or textile paints and colors are now available which can be safely used by children. These pillows were stuffed with kapok, though foam pellets or polyester batting also work well.

Needlepoint Doll

A joint effort between a mother and her son produced this delightful doll: a marvelous gift for the new baby. Perhaps most important of all is the attention given by the mother to the older child and his drawing so that the boy shares in the excitement.

The straightforward drawing was transferred from paper to canvas and sewn in needlepoint stitches. Children's drawings often adapt readily to other materials and to a variety of projects.

Needlepoint doll, sewn by Diana Van Wagoner Speer from a drawing of her son's.

A boy's drawing was
the inspiration for this
doll by Betsy Mitchell.
Ten inches tall.

Halloween Boy

The Halloween figure, another drawing by a small boy, was transferred to fabric, sewn, and stuffed. It's very exciting for a child to watch his drawing turn into a stuffed "real" object.

The different-colored materials for the shirt and pants were first pieced together, then the body shape was cut from that pieced fabric. Features were embroidered. Yarn hair and a felt hat complete the figure.

Brothers, easily made from felt, include the older child in a gift to the new one.

Brother/Sister Dolls

All gifts need not be for the baby. Why not make a *pair* of dolls, one large and one small, so the older child can keep the big one and give the little one to the baby?

Here are two sets: a boy along with a smaller brother, and the girl with a little sister. Obviously, a brother/sister combination can also be used. The large dolls here are seventeen inches tall and the smaller ones are thirteen and a half inches tall. If there are more children in the family, just change the length of legs to suggest various heights or different ages.

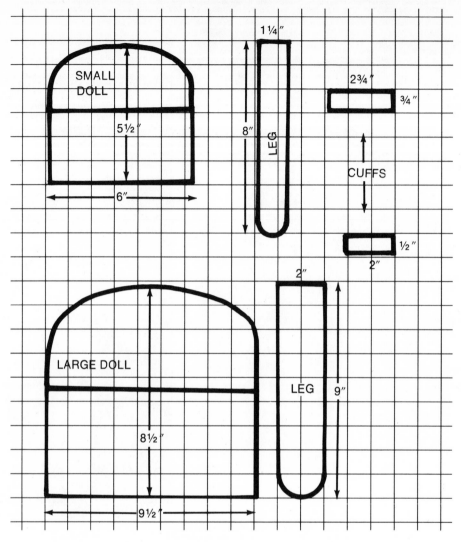

Cut the felt doll parts as shown in the pattern on the grid. If woven materials are used, be sure to add seam allowances. Felt can be top-stitched on the right side. Sew all the appliqué pieces to the large body shape, including the arms and the faces. Join legs in pairs so that each leg is double thickness. Repeat for arms. Join the front and back body pieces, starting on one side. Sew one side, inserting the arm. Insert legs in the seam at the bottom, then the second arm. When only the top of the head is left open, stuff the doll with Dacron batting, then finish sewing. Finally, add ball fringe for hair. Use the ball fringe that comes in a row of connected balls rather than the kind joined to a tape by strings. If you have to use the latter, cut off the individual balls and sew them singly to the felt doll.

Colors for the hair, eyes, or clothes can be selected to fit the child for whom the doll is made. The addition of the child's name would be a welcome touch.

The amounts of ribbon and edging used are small, so you can probably vary the decorative details according to what trims you have available.

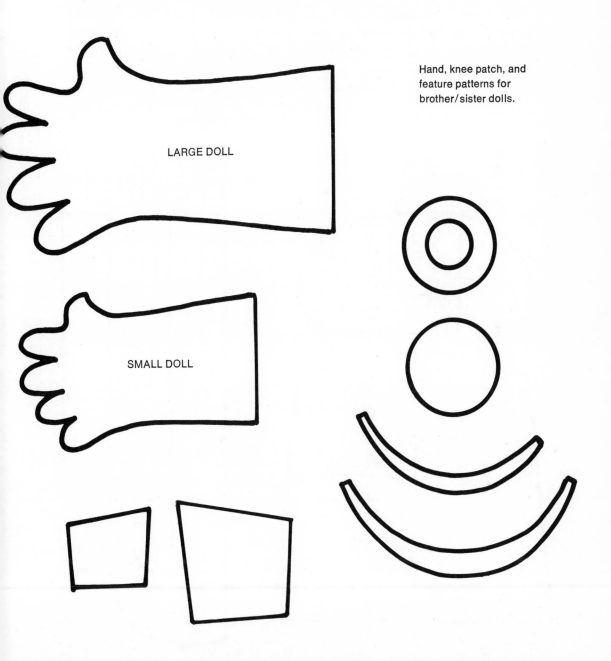

LARGE DOLL

SMALL DOLL

Hand, knee patch, and feature patterns for brother/sister dolls.

Buttons, edgings, or laces from the clothes of parents, grandparents, aunts, uncles, cousins, friends, and (most particularly) from the child's own clothes, add to the fun.

Batik Doll

This charming doll is made using a wax-resist process to suggest all the face and clothing details. Anyone familiar with batik will especially enjoy them. And they can be made as big sister/little sister dolls for another possible way of assuring that the older child feels included in all the excitement of a new arrival.

The pattern for the batik doll can be used for dolls decorated in any of a number of other ways. Direct painting with acrylics or dyes will give

Pattern for batik doll. (1 square = 1 inch)

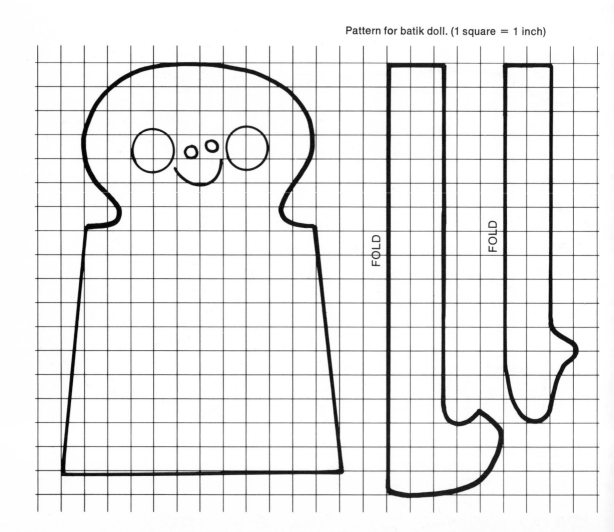

Batik doll by Nancy Taylor is irresistible and will probably disappear from the nursery unless another is made for the sibling.

Detail shows the way
that hair is added to
Nancy Taylor's doll.

a similar pattern effect on the fabric. Appliqué, embroidery, and ball-point markers are equally appropriate.

The pattern can be enlarged to whatever size is preferred. Add seam allowance, then machine-sew seams and turn right side out. Hair of yarn is added.

5. gifts for new parents or grandparents

The arrival of the baby offers an opportunity to make gifts for the new parents and the grandparents. Certainly not *all* of the attention needs to be lavished on the child, who, after all, remains somewhat oblivious to the gifts for some time. If it is a friend of yours who is about to become a mother or a grandmother, certainly she is the one you may want to present with a gift to highlight the occasion. Following are gift ideas which are appropriate for parents or grandparents.

Feeding Set

It is sometimes helpful for grandparents to have on hand some of the basic necessities, so that when grandchildren come to visit, everything is ready. One gift of this kind is a feeding set.

This one consists of three pieces, each made of cotton gingham and lined in a cherry pink vinyl. The lap pad is cut 18 inches by 22 inches (46 cm by 56 cm) with rounded corners, and is bound with a woven binding. The flowers made from the drawing on the grid are applied with machine

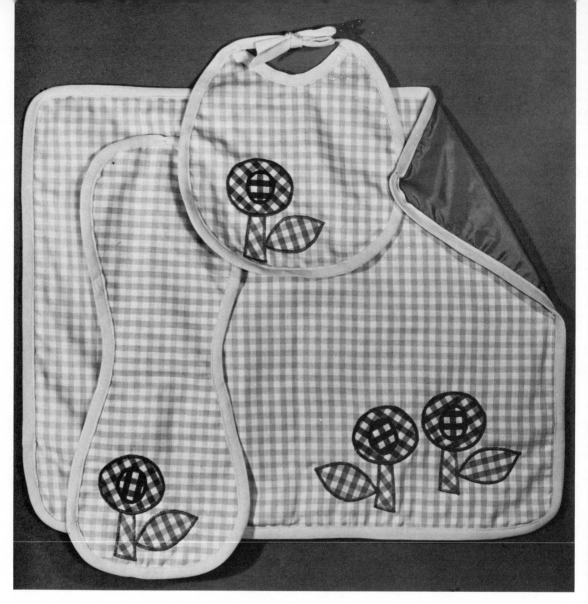

Gingham feeding set has lap pad, bib, and a burping cloth.

appliqué before lining. The flowers are adhered with a fabric bonding adhesive which adds some stiffening. Then the raw edges are satin-stitched with bright-colored threads.

The burp pad is 18 inches (46 cm) long and is 8 inches (20 cm) wide at the ends, but only 5 inches (13 cm) wide at the center. It goes over the shoulder before burping the baby. It keeps the tiny drips of curdled milk off Grandmother's new dress. It is appliquéd, lined, and bound in the same

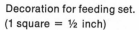

Decoration for feeding set.
(1 square = ½ inch)

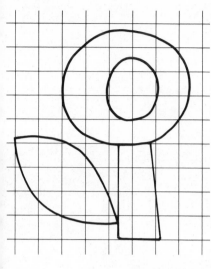

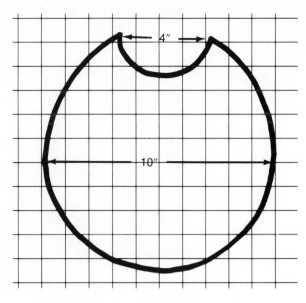

← 4" →

10"

Feeding set—bib and burp pad. (1 square = 1 inch)

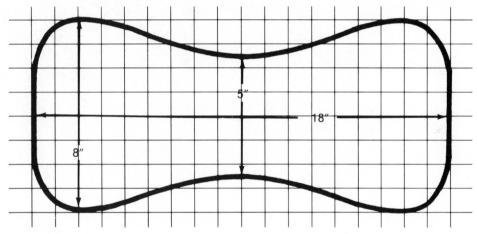

5"

18"

8"

way as the lap pad. The bib, which is 10 inches (25 cm) wide, completes the set.

Place Mats, Napkins, and Napkin Rings

Special place mats for a small child make even a snack seem special. Use washable cotton fabrics, piecing various colors together with prints for a bright pattern effect.

These mats are around 16 inches long and they vary in width from 12 inches to 14 inches. When the top of the mat has been pieced, and the ribbons or edgings machine-stitched in place, add a backing fabric. This can be any related color, cut the same size as the finished mat. Place right sides together and sew around three sides and the four corners. Turn, then use slip stitch to close the opening to complete the mat.

Napkins, made the same way, may vary in size. These are 10 inches square and have design motifs similar to the mats.

Napkin rings are made from two strips of material cut 2½ inches by 8 inches (6.4 cm by 20 cm), plus seam allowance. One strip is decorated with edgings. They are sewn in the same way as the napkin, then turned and slip-stitched. One end of the finished band is overlapped about ¾ of

Place mats with matching napkins and napkin rings, make lunch at Grandmother's a special treat.

Napkin ring assembled

an inch (10 mm) over the other, making the ring, as in the drawing. Ends are top-stitched or slip-stitched. If the materials used in this set are soft, use an interfacing or stiffening on the inside of the napkin rings. These, made with cotton fabrics and cotton edgings, required no additional liner.

Place mats can also be decorated in the same way as the feeding set, using machine appliqué. Any of the drawings given in the book may be used on place mats. If you are appliquéing them by hand, add a seam allowance.

Baby carrier was decorated with a sunburst design with an allover stitching pattern in the background. By Nina Stull.

Baby Carrier

Baby carriers are a tremendous aid to young parents who don't intend to hibernate while the babies are small. They are helpful to the mother with another small child and almost indispensable for errands and shopping when the baby accompanies the parent. Many have plain panels which invite decorative additions. In the decorative design done on the carrier in the photograph, the background was filled with a filigree pattern of machine stitching. The drawings may give you other ideas.

Motifs for baby carriers

A Two-Piece Baby Carrier

Another simple and very comfortable baby carrier is shown in these drawings. The baby's legs come through the open ends of the shoulder strap which also forms the sides of the bag. Be sure to use a good strong fabric—sailcloth, light canvas, or heavy denim—and double-stitch all seams.

To make this two-piece carrier, cut a strip of strong fabric 15 inches by approximately 54 inches (38 cm by 137 cm) long. Sew lengthwise, turn, and top-stitch so that the strip finishes at 7 inches by 54 inches (18 cm by 137 cm). The length of the shoulder strap varies according to the height of the carrier, how high on the hip the baby is held, and whether the shoulder strap is crossed over the head to the opposite shoulder.

Next cut a rectangle 24 inches by 7 inches (61 cm by 18 cm) for the

Two-piece baby carrier

SHOULDER STRAP

CENTER PANEL

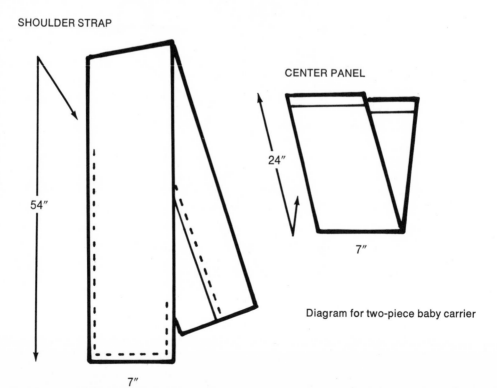

54"

7"

24"

7"

Diagram for two-piece baby carrier

center panel. Either double the piece or line it. Fold this piece crosswise and bind all the ends as shown in the drawing. Then assemble, joining line A–B of the shoulder strap to A–B of the center panel. Repeat for lines C–D. Then sew the second side the same way.

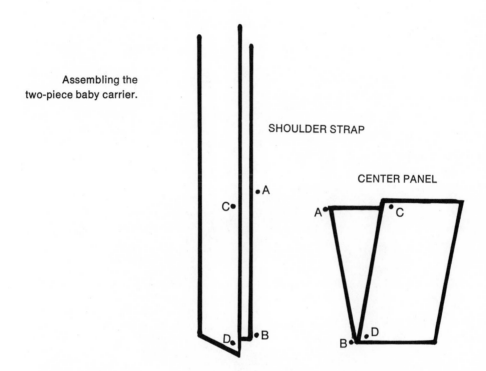

Assembling the two-piece baby carrier.

Add any decorative appliqué to the center panel before the parts are assembled.

Photo Album

A photo album is definitely an essential item for parents or grandparents, especially for a second or third child. It seems that endless quantities of photos are always made of the first child. When the next ones arrive, there isn't a free hand to carry the camera! An album may serve as a gentle reminder to expose the film.

This album, featuring a snapshot of the baby, is simply a fabric cover made for a purchased book-type album. It can be hand-sewn, or the end folds can be machine-stitched, then slipped over the book's cover.

A printed-fabric photograph-album cover has iron-on tape lettering with embroidery. The heart with a cutout in the middle is appliquéd over a photograph.

The easiest kind of album to cover with fabric is one which has separate removable covers with a string or cord that runs through the eyelets to secure the covers. This type of album is covered by first removing the front and back covers and then stitching the fabric cover over them, and then reassembling the album as shown in the drawing.

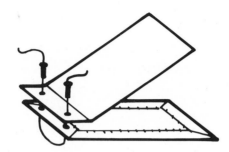

Simple type of photo album

Any type of needlework can be used for either of these basic book-covering methods. Appliqué, crewel stitchery, needlepoint, and even quilting are all suitable. Small purse-sized photo albums are covered in the same way.

Pincushions

A few nurseries are still equipped with nondisposable diapers, and those require not only pins but pincushions. Here are a few that are not merely functional but beautiful as well. These serve to show off some choice pieces of family needle lace and a doily. Any mother would enjoy them.

Cotton velveteen makes a luxurious cushion, and the dull sheen combines beautifully with the linear design of laces. If you are using antique needlework, measure each piece to determine the correct size of the backing fabric. Squares, circles, or ovals are all appropriate. Allow a minimum of ½ of an inch (13 mm) all the way around lace or needlework plus the seam allowance. If you are using a circular doily, cut the circle of velveteen either larger or smaller than the doily. If you cut it larger, the doily is simply centered on the circle. If the velveteen is cut smaller, then the doily can be used to wrap around the cushion and cover the seam, as in the example shown. The square pincushions both have needlework that is smaller than the square of fabric on which it is mounted.

Place right sides of the fabric together. Sew a little more than three-quarters of the way around. On the squares, machine-sew all four corners. Then turn right side out, stuff with steel wool or sawdust, and close the opening with slip stitches. Finally, attach the doily with small white tacking stitches.

This method of dressing up pincushions can also be used with store-bought or old pincushions. Simply make a new cover of velveteen but allow a larger opening when you sew it so the pincushion can be inserted into its new case.

Use special pieces of lace or one of Great-grandmother's doilies for these exquisite pincushions. Four inches to five inches across.

House Lap Pad

Every grandparent needs a lap pad for protection from the wet spots which a baby inevitably leaves. An elegant patchwork lap pad is shown here. The design could be expanded to make a quilt, though this size (13½ inches by 19 inches [34 cm by 48 cm]) is perfect for lap use.

The blocks are first cut according to the pattern on the grid and joined with machine or hand stitching. Be sure to add seam allowances to all edges. The blocks should be assembled in rows, going across. Then the rows can be joined. By assembling the blocks this way, only straight lines have to be sewn.

As the blocks are joined, the seams should be pressed. Either press seams open, or press them all in one direction. Then add the appliqué pieces, again adding seam allowances, and decorate them with a few lines of embroidery. Two strands of cotton embroidery floss were used here. For the appliqué, regular sewing thread was used.

When the top is finished, a second piece of fabric or backing is cut to

House lap pad. (1 square = 1 inch)

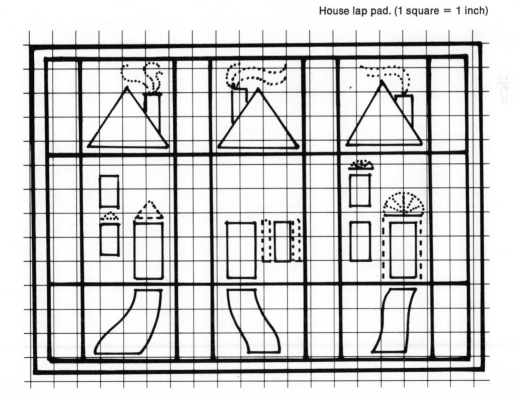

House lap pad, with appliqué details, has an absorbent filler.

the same dimensions. Two or three layers of flannel, used as filler, are also cut to that size. (A flannel blanket can be cut up, or a used cotton sheet-blanket will provide a good filler.) The important thing is that the pad must be absorbent if it is to function. The rubberized lap pads available in department stores are hard to sew through by hand, so avoid them if you intend to quilt by hand. If you quilt by machine, or decide not to quilt the pad at all, the flannelized rubber pads will work well.

Place the backing fabric, right side down, on a table. Place the flannel or rubber pad over that, then the pieced material, right side up. Baste at the outside edges.

If no quilting is to be done, simply bind the raw edges using strips of fabric cut 1½ inches (38 cm) wide, plus seam allowance.

If you intend to quilt by machine, the basting at the outside edge should be secure. Then machine-stitch exactly on the seam lines between the blocks. When quilting is finished, proceed with binding as described above. If you intend to quilt by hand, follow the directions given on quilting on page 181.

Any quilt block pattern can be adapted for use as a lap pad. Simply make enough blocks to cover the lap amply and quilt them with a backing. It can later be used by the child as a blanket for a doll or a teddy bear.

Grandfather's Lap Pad

This pad is made in the manner of the beautiful Amish quilts—a kind of miniature version. The colors are close in range—wines, deep blues and reds—and strong, and the pad is of ample proportions.

Velveteen adds an elegant sheen to this top. (It's the washable cotton

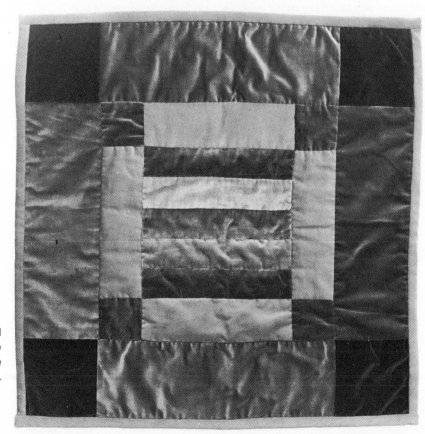

Grandfather's lap pad is of velveteen in a simple pattern and ample proportions.

variety.) It is padded and backed, observing the same functional considerations as those for the house lap pad. This lap pad is twenty-six inches square, though obviously other sizes and proportions would do as well. This pad, too, may take on a new life later when it becomes a doll blanket or floor pad. It also serves well as a car pad for the baby.

Quilted Carryall

A quilted and padded carryall bag is perfect for keeping milk bottles or baby foods warm on an outing. This one is simple to make and easy to carry.

To start with, a pieced top, 24 inches (61 cm) square, is made. A simple pieced repeat pattern works well since the pattern is interrupted

Quilted carryall with pockets is thick enough to keep bottles and baby foods warm.

with zippers. However, a printed fabric will work nicely. Start out with the fabric pieces an inch or two larger since the quilting will decrease the size slightly. Place backing fabric facedown on a flat surface. (This will later be the lining of the pockets.) Put a layer of filler over this. A piece of Dacron blanket, one or two layers of flannel, or any insulating fabric will do. Place the printed or pieced fabric, faceup, on top of that. Pin, baste, and quilt. Next, trim the edges so that all are straight, then bind the edges with a matching material.

Fold two sides to the center to determine where pockets should go. Mark openings with pins. If necessary, measure over bottles or jars of baby food, but for most containers an opening of around 4 inches is adequate. A zipper will have to be slightly longer than that since it does not open all the way to either end. If it is not possible to find short zippers, such as the zippers made for dolls' clothes, use longer plastic ones and cut them off to the desired length.

Pockets in this carryall were sewn according to the diagram. Cut the 6 openings as shown. With the material flat, it will be easy to set in zippers or to bind the openings. Use a bound buttonhole opening, or simply bind the cut edges with bias tape or bias-cut fabric. When all the openings have been finished, fold the sides to the center. Machine-stitch or hand-stitch top and bottom, down the center, and between pockets.

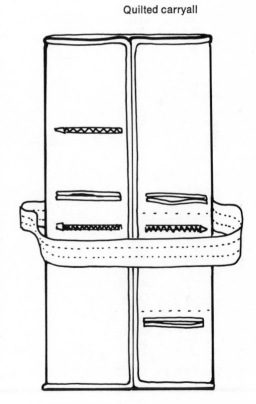

Quilted carryall

The handle of this bag is cut 22 inches long by 5 inches (56 cm by 13 cm) wide. It is doubled, reinforced with a stiff interfacing, and top-stitched with three lines of machine sewing. One inch at each end is turned back so that the handle is double where it joins the bag.

Pockets are on the outside of the bag for easy access to spoons, napkins, or bottles. The bag can be reversed so that zippers go to the underside and do not show.

6. for play

It has often been observed that babies provide a wonderful excuse for adults to buy the toys they'd like to have themselves. If so, it is evidence of the child in us all. Without doubt, there is a special pleasure in making and giving toys. Perhaps it's a way of reexperiencing the fun of making new discoveries!

Swing

This delightful needlepoint swing for a toddler, by Nancy Welch, is in a combination of yellow, pink, orange, and turquoise. It is worked on interlocked needlepoint canvas (7 to the inch) which has been doubled to form a panel 6 inches by 14 inches (15 cm by 36 cm). This makes it extra firm and strong. The ends of the panel were folded and stitched to leave an open area 2½ inches (6.4 cm) wide where the rope could be inserted. The canvas was folded back under the swing and the needlepoint stitches went through both layers of canvas. The drawing shows the construction.

An enticing swing combines needlepoint, knotting, and wrapping. By Nancy Welch.

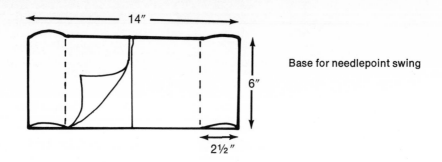

Base for needlepoint swing

The ropes (⅜ of an inch [10 mm] in diameter) are wrapped with yarn, crossed, and spliced together several feet above the swing seat. If you don't have a resident knot-tying sailor, you can tie the ends of the rope over the branch or beam where you install the swing.

The fringe at the sides is thick and full—the result of two different steps. The needlepoint yarns were drawn to the ends as the work progressed. Each time a new color was added, the tail of the last yarn was pulled out to the edge. Then, when the needlepoint was finished, additional rya knots were tied onto the edge to finish the canvas and fringe. Tassels and bells add the final bonuses of movement and sound.

This swing is designed to be good and sturdy and should be set low to the ground. A similar swing could be made using any strong fabric, such as awning canvas, and appliquéing designs to the cloth. Weaving, macrame, or painted fabric, all offer possibilities for a swing to let any child enjoy the pleasures of swinging—indoors or out.

For the indoor swing, if no exposed beam is available, use large eyebolts which can be fixed into a doorway. These can be installed to be strong enough to hold the baby as well as any adult with an urge to go "up in the air so blue."

Bouncing Doll

Hung on an elastic cord, this bean-filled doll will dance endlessly. It is ideal over crib or basket where a baby's hand can touch it to set it in bouncing motion.

The basic doll form is made with a cotton sock. Stuff the toe and foot with Dacron batting just past the heel. Then tie off to suggest a head, as

Bouncing doll

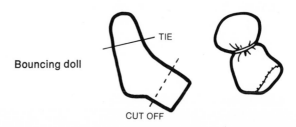

Bean-stuffed doll bounces endlessly on an elastic string.

shown in the drawing. Cut the cuff of the sock off and sew the open end shut. From printed fabric cut two arm pieces 2¾ inches by 5½ inches (7 cm by 14 cm). Fold lengthwise and sew one side, ending with a curve at one end. Turn.

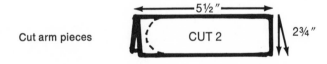

Cut arm pieces — 5½" — CUT 2 — 2¾"

The suit is made from two pieces of fabric cut 8 inches by 7 inches (20 cm by 18 cm). Fold over 1 inch (25 mm) on the wrong side of one 7-inch edge, and use iron-on tape to finish the raw edge. Place right sides of front and back together. Pin. Slip arms to the inside. Stitch sides and bottom, catching arms in place with the seam. This part of the doll can be varied by piecing it from various fabrics as the one in the photograph was, or by adding decorative edgings or ribbons. If buttons, bells, or other

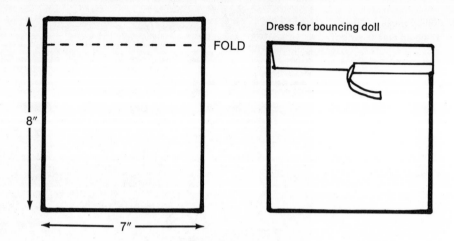

FOLD

8"

7"

Dress for bouncing doll

objects are used, special care must be taken to secure them in such a way that a baby will not be able to pull them off or put them in his or her mouth.

Next, use a heavy cord, buttonhole twist, or some sturdy doubled thread to sew a running stitch about 1 inch from the top finished edge. Leave long ends on the cord. This will form the collar and join the body to the head. Put dry beans in this bag, then slip the stocking body inside and pull the string tight and tie. If it is tight and correctly placed, sew additional stitches to secure these parts. Some additional tying will assure that the parts will not separate (thus releasing the beans). Use fabric glue or stitches to add the felt features to the stocking face.

The hair is made by cutting a felt circle approximately 10 inches in diameter. Sew elastic cord to the top of the doll's head. Attach securely.

Features for bouncing doll

Cut a tiny hole in the felt, and slide it down over the elastic to sit on the doll's head. Attach with glue or stitches. Then clip the felt away to suggest hair and bangs. Cuts are made from the outside edge toward the center. Hang the doll by its elastic cord above the crib for hours of entertainment.

The Flying Trapeze Man

Here is a clown to perform acrobatics to amuse the playful of all ages. The basic body is made from a stuffed sock, in the same way used for the bouncing doll. Arms, legs, and shirt are shown in the drawing. Add seam allowances at all edges. Each arm and leg is folded as shown and seamed on the long side, then turned. The patterns for the hands and feet are full size. They should be felt. Doubling each will make them stiff enough to hold their shape. The double layers can be sewed or glued together. No seam allowance is needed on the felt pieces. The hands and feet are slipped into place at the ends of the arms and legs so that the raw edge of the fabric folds down over the felt. Whipstitch or top-stitch the ends so that parts are securely fastened.

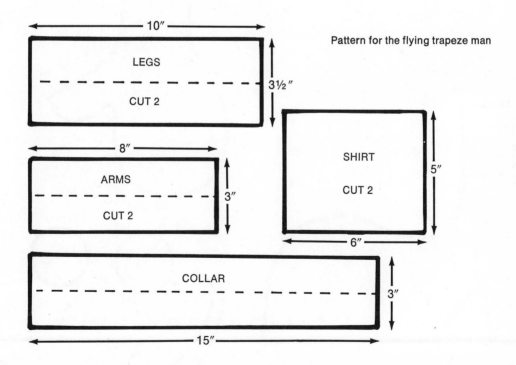

Pattern for the flying trapeze man

Arms and legs are lightly stuffed and then sewn into the side and bottom seams of the polka-dot shirt. The sock is slipped into the shirt and the two are hand-stitched securely together at the neck.

The ruff or collar is gathered and tied around the neck. The felt features are glued or sewn in place, as is the ball fringe nose. Hair of yarn is stitched to the stuffed head. A clown hat adds the final touch. Be sure to make a paper hat first, as the size needed will vary according to the size of the sock and the amount of stuffing in it.

When the clown is assembled, sew Velcro dots to the palm and sleeve of each arm. With these the clown can keep his grasp by wrapping the hand around the rope or ring and snapping the Velcro dots together. Plastic rings tied to cotton cord, or a short piece of dowel or plastic rod tied to the same cord, give the clown a trapeze on which to perform his amazing feats. Additional Velcro dots on his shoes and legs allow him to hang by his feet. A line of stitching across the middle of each leg will form a knee, allowing the leg to bend. Velcro dots added there would let him swing by his knees.

Flying trapeze man—feet, hands, and features

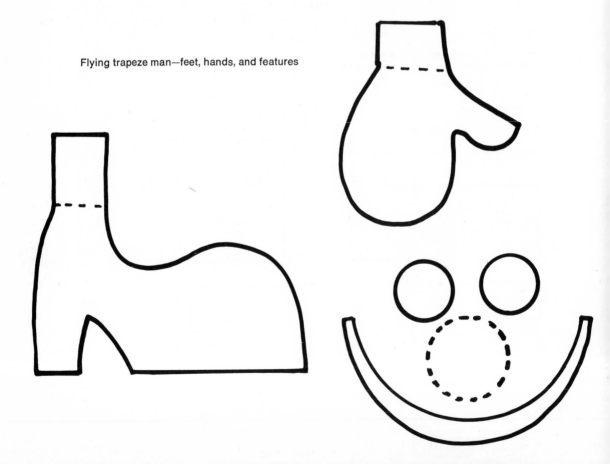

The flying trapeze man hangs from Velcro hands. Twenty-four inches tall.

This very versatile performer can come down from his perch to be played with as a stuffed toy as well. The trapeze is dispensable—he is as happy to be hanging over the edge of a crib or playpen.

Woven Doll

Weaving will not be the fastest way of making this doll, but for the weaver it may be the most enjoyable. The pattern is simple and can be used with any sturdy fabric. Parts are made separately and joined.

When you cut the pattern, add seam allowances to all edges. When the leg pieces are cut and sewn, they are stuffed with polyester or cotton batting. Then the body parts are placed, face sides together, so that the legs are caught in the seam. Arms and head are added separately.

If the doll is to be made from yardage fabrics, join the colors for the head and body first. Then cut those parts in one piece, as shown. Do the same for the legs and shoes. When all parts are assembled, embroider the features with yarn. The hair consists of tufts of yarn tied together. Then the ties are sewn to the fabric and the yarns are fluffed out.

The dress on this doll was done with a latch hook, but if you are using a more finely woven fabric, the woven loops can be stitched on.

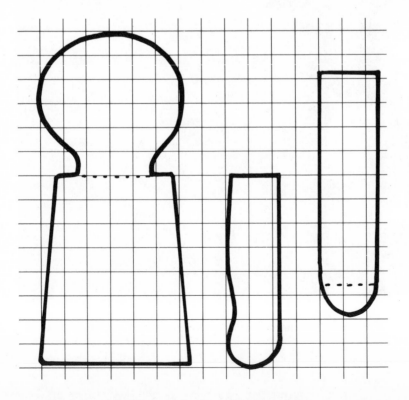

Woven doll pattern.
(1 square = 1 inch)

A handwoven doll, twenty-two inches tall, by Olga Seeley.

Stuffed fabric doll, thirteen inches tall, has a hairdo of unspun wool. By Bets Barnard.

Bets' Doll

This pretty little fabric doll is sturdy, lovable, and easy to hold. While the yarn hair is not best for the baby who is still mouthing everything, the toddler will love its softness, as well as the movements of the doll's legs.

Plain-weave fabrics, such as kettle cloth, muslin, and cotton twill, work well. The shoe fabric is pieced to the leg fabric before the leg shape is cut and sewn. The features are hand-stitched bits of felt. Unspun wool,

Pattern for Bets' doll.
(1 square = 1 inch)

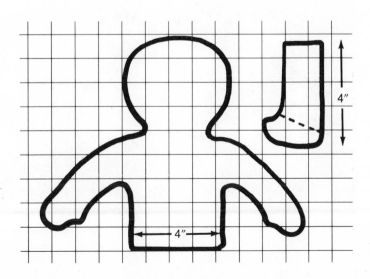

twisted into coils and curls, is stitched to the head for a fashionable hairdo. The dress is made from two squares of fabric; the finished size is 5 inches by 5 inches (13 cm by 13 cm). Add seam allowances, then join at the sides, leaving the top half of each side open for the arm. Finish raw edges of the armhole and hem. Fold over ¼ of an inch (6 mm) at the top edge and stitch with ⅛-inch (3-mm) elastic tape on the inside of the fold. Use a 6-inch (15-cm) length of elastic. Tie at the waist with a ribbon.

Sock Dolls

Made from white stretch gym socks, in as large a size as can be found, these well-stuffed babies are inexpensive and simple to make.

Start by stuffing the toe and foot of the sock. Let the heel form the baby's seat. Cut off some of the cuff of the sock and reserve that portion for arms as in the diagram. When the end of the cuff has been removed,

Twin dolls, made from a pair of gym socks, are the creation of Karen Jahncke.

slit the remaining part to form the two legs which will poke out directly in front. Slip-stitch shut, being sure to finish stuffing as you go. Sew the cuff as shown into two arm shapes. Slip-stitch in place. Tie the sock to suggest a neck and to form the head.

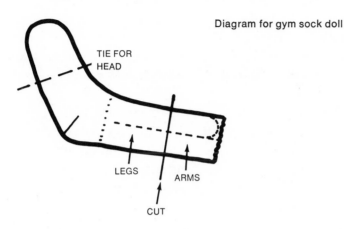

Diagram for gym sock doll

Features are felt, either stitched or glued in place. Rouge is patted lightly onto the fabric to add pink cheeks and chin. Yarn is tacked in loops onto the head.

If this doll is stuffed with Dacron or polyester, and if nylon yarn is used for the hair, it is washable. The felt features should be removed and sewn back on after washing.

Wynken, Blynken, and Nod Dolls

Any child delights in having a bed to put the dollies in. And small dolls make it easy to find beds. Cardboard boxes and bread pans are the favorites of many children. Here,

> Wynken, Blynken and Nod one night
> Sailed off in a wooden shoe—
> Sailed on a river of crystal light
> Into a sea of dew.

These tiny dolls delight toddlers. Make several, and then make some little beds to keep them in.

The dolls are made of cotton fabric and the pattern is the exact size. Add seam allowance at all edges. Two identical pieces, placed with right sides together, are joined except for an opening at the side. This allows for the fabric to be turned right side out. Stuffing is added and the opening is closed with overcast stitches. French knots make eyes, and a row of outline stitches forms the mouth. Nylon yarn is used for the hair.

The dress is a piece of fabric cut 7 inches by 2½ inches (18 cm by 6.4 cm). The fabric wraps around the doll and slits are cut in the sides for the arms. The neck is gathered and stitched together or snapped at the back. Add trims or edgings as desired. A tiny patchwork quilt accompanies the dolls to bed.

A simple method for making a little bed, possibly of fabric that matches the nightie or dress, is that used in making a bunting. Cut a miniature version of those shown in chapter 7. The bunting or bed needs a little additional stuffing at the top to suggest a pillow.

Pattern for Wynken, Blynken, and Nod dolls

Two tiny dolls are tucked into a wooden shoe bed with their miniature quilt. By Karen Jahncke.

115

Leather Cat

Tiny scraps of leather provide enough material for small, childproof stuffed toys. This fat little cat is machine-sewn at the outside edge. The ears and the tail, just a single thickness, are caught in the seam as the

Leather cat pattern

A sturdy leather cat, just four and one-half inches high, is machine-sewn. By Melanie Fogle.

front and back parts are joined. Some leather workers find it helpful to glue the leather first (using leather cement) and then stitch, trimming the edge of the leather right next to the stitching.

The face is drawn in with India ink, but eyes and nose are tiny dots of leather cut out with a leather punch. The bow tied around the neck is a single strip of leather. The pattern here is full size. Cut a tail around 2½ inches long.

Menagerie

A whole ark full of animals can be made by applying dye or paint directly to the surface of cloth. This collection is silk-screened, and anyone

familiar with the process could turn out herds of animals in an afternoon.
Direct dye painting can also be used. In that, dyes are brushed onto the
fabric and are set. In any of these methods the printed shape is then cut
out in a simplified form. This form is backed with another colored fabric
and the two are stitched and stuffed.

Marking pens and ball-point fabric markers provide the easiest
method of direct dye work. See page 186 for additional information on

These animals were silk-screened on muslin by Tyna and Wayne Donelson.

118   their use. Acrylic paints can also be applied directly to fabrics. Older children will enjoy making toys for a new baby by using this method. They can work directly on the stretched fabric, or do drawings on paper to be transferred to cloth.

Hen and Eggs

This surprise toy is a favorite of babies who delight in endlessly putting eggs in and taking them out. The hen's wings lift up to reveal openings through which the eggs are removed and replaced.

When you cut the patterns, add seam allowances to all pieces cut from woven fabric, but not on any pieces cut from felt, except the wings. A combination can be used, as it was in this printed fabric hen where felt for comb, tail, and beak were used. A lining material is also needed. Any quilted or somewhat stiff fabric makes the hen perch more alertly on her nest. With too soft a fabric she will sink abjectly over her eggs.

Pattern for hen and eggs. (1 square = 1 inch)

TUCKS

CUT 2

CUT OUT

BEAK

EYE

COMB

↑ GATHER THIS EDGE

TAILS

WING

OVAL BASE

EGG

Hen and eggs, a stitched and padded toy by Nina Stull.

Place one side of the hen and its lining with right sides together and sew around the center opening. Turn and top-stitch around the opening. Repeat for other side. Then, with right sides together, join fabric and lining for wings. Turn, then top-stitch the outside edge. Stitch the wing to the side of the hen by turning the wing to point up. Top-stitch just above the opening so that when the wing is dropped, it covers the seam and the hole. Sew eye in place. Take tucks at the top edge of the hen's back, then with right sides together, join the two side sections which form the hen. Join over back, top, and front, leaving bottom open, and being sure to catch beak, comb, and tail in the outside seam.

Next take tucks in the bottom edge of the hen shapes at each side. Then sew the bottom opening to the oval, easing in any extra fullness in the fabric. Turn right side out through the wing hole.

To form eggs, take tucks in the ovals where shown. Then join two shapes, right sides together, leaving an opening to turn the egg right side

120 out. Stuff and slip-stitch shut. If you decorate eggs, it is much easier to do that before taking tucks or assembling the two pieces.

If there are older children in the family, plan to make at least two hens. This is one of those baby toys which siblings find irresistible.

Four-inch squares of felt are cut and appliquéd, ready to be assembled, to make a cube.

Soft Blocks

Almost any decorative fabric method can be used in making soft blocks for children. Embroidery, needlepoint, marking pens, crewel stitching, appliqué, and quilting are all suitable.

The blocks shown here are made of felt appliqué and stuffed with polyester. Each felt square is cut 4 inches by 4 inches (10 cm by 10 cm). The appliqué designs are added and then the parts are joined by stitching. It requires 6 squares to make a cube. Some design suggestions are shown in full size on the next page. If

Soft blocks, whipstitched together, are stuffed with batting.

these are used for fabric appliqué instead of felt, be sure to add an allowance to be turned under.

Design ideas for soft blocks

Doll bag has an open mind and
an amazing capacity for objects.
By Bonnie Floyd.

Lucy Locket's Pocket

This little doll opens her head to become a purse! To make her, add seam allowances to all pattern pieces. First cut out and sew the feet and hands according to the pattern which is full size, stuffing them with a little batting. Then cut four faces, two pink for the front section and two yellow for the back, according to the pattern on the grid. Sew one of the pink faces to the dress front, gathering fullness at top of dress. Sew a yellow face to the dress back, again gathering the top edge. Then place

Lucy Locket's pocket—hand and foot.

HAND

FOOT

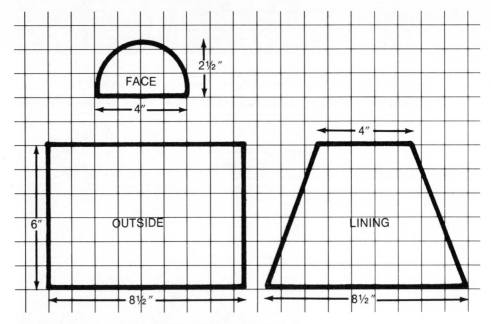

Pattern for Lucy Locket's pocket. (1 square = 1 inch)

the dress-lining pieces together and join at both sides and at the bottom. Join dress front to dress back this same way, being sure to insert the stuffed hands and feet to catch them in the seam. Finally place the second yellow face on the first, right sides together, and sew over the top of the arch but not across the base. Turn. Repeat for the front, matching the second pink face over the first. Turn.

Next cut two cardboard pieces the same size as the face pattern but do not add a seam allowance. Trim if necessary to make the cardboard pieces fit between the face shapes of the front and the back. Add a little Dacron batting between the cardboard and the front pink face. This will round out the face.

Slip-stitch the dress-lining pieces to the face-lining pieces. The face may be added in any of several ways. Fabric appliqué, felt appliqué, embroidery, or marking pen will work. This one is painted with acrylic paint using the flat end of a pencil eraser as a stamp. Two blue dots for eyes and two pink ones for cheeks. A red painted line makes the mouth.

Yarn can be tied or braided and tack-stitched to the face on the front side. Add ribbons or yarn ties. A ribbon or cord is added to the top back

Acrylic stamping was used for Lucy Lockett's eyes and cheeks.

piece to become a handle. A tiny loop of elastic cord with a corresponding button on the opposite side is added as a closure for the bag.

Counting Book

This fabric book is full of ideas and things to do. The appliqués are machine-stitched felt on a woven cloth backing.

The full pages are cut 23 inches by 11 inches (58 cm by 28 cm). The appliqué is finished before the pages are joined. For a 14-page book, plus front and back covers, 8 rectangles of that size are needed. Pages are joined back to back, and each double fabric provides two pages. If pages are to be numbered, it will be important to plan the arrangement carefully. A paper mock-up of the book will be very helpful.

Nina Stull's delightful counting book
has parts that move up and down, on and off, in and out.

127

After the appliqué is completed, the pages are placed together and are bound with wide bias tape. The drawings show how pages are bound and joined.

Binding the counting book's
pages with tape

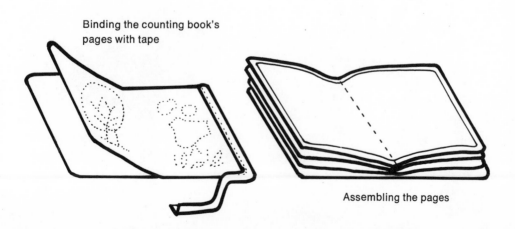

Assembling the pages

The little bear's coverlet moves up and down.

The concepts in this book are those of contrast. In open/closed, for example, the words appear, then there is a frog with a mouth that lifts open. In on/off, the flowers are put on or off the tree with Velcro dots. Inventive appliqués occur all the way through the book. Most mothers will want to use those objects with which her child is familiar.

Batik dolls are the creations of
Nancy Taylor. (Photo
by Gayle Smalley)

The flying trapeze man has Velcro on his hands to aid in
his acrobatics. (Photo by Stan Bitters)

A colorful pieced and
appliquéd pad for the lap
of visiting relatives who
want to hold the baby.
(Photo by Gayle Smalley)

This curly-headed doll is made from handwoven fabric. By Olga Seeley. (Photo by Gayle Smalley)

Calico hen has felt-lined wings which lift to reveal a whole nest of embroidered eggs. By Nina Stull. (Photo by Gayle Smalley)

Nina Stull's fabric book uses bright colored felts on a sturdy brushed cotton. (Photo by Gayle Smalley)

Picture Book

Another fabric book utilizes washable cottons to make the material childproof. The same procedure is used. Individual appliqués are sewn first, then pages are joined and bound with tape. Any of the drawings in this book could be used on fabric pages of this type.

Fabric appliqué provides colorful designs in this washable book.

A giant picture book, for example one with pages two feet square, would delight any crawler who could turn the giant pages. And little four-inch books have a charm of their own. Certainly they travel easily.

This book's pages are twelve inches high.

7. going out

One of the pleasures of "going out" is to introduce the new baby to the rest of the world. And here is where needlework gifts come into their own, offering an opportunity to combine function with an extravagance of color. And perhaps an opportunity to show off some special talents for needlework.

Quilted Bunting

Here is an elegant bunting to take the baby visiting. The dimensions can be varied, but this size is good up to about one year.

First cut the front panel 21 inches by 22 inches (53 cm by 56 cm) and the backing panel 36 inches by 22 inches (92 cm by 56 cm) as shown in the diagram. Cut two of each—one color for the inside and a contrasting color for the outside. Here, the outside fabrics are white with a spring green for the inside. Round off the top corners of the larger rectangle. By folding the back in half lengthwise, it is possible to assure that the curve is identical on the two sides.

The next step is to appliqué a quilt block to the outside color of the

Quilted bunting has a gloriously bright appliqué block on the front panel.

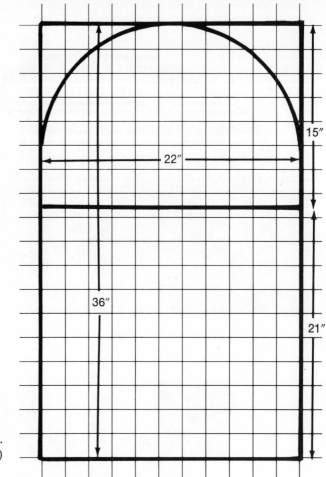

22″

15″

36″

21″

Quilted bunting.
(1 square = 2 inches)

front panel. This can be an old quilt block, either pieced or appliquéd, or you can appliqué the design shown here.

   . This appliquéd quilt block is 16 inches (41 cm) square finished. The large outside circle in the center is 5¼ inches (13 cm) in diameter; the next is 3¼ inches (8 cm). All other pieces for this design are shown in the drawing on the grid. Pin pieces onto the quilt block and appliqué in place. Use a running stitch, sewing with a single strand of sewing thread. Add seam allowance, and turn under the raw edge as you sew. When the design has been appliquéd, sew the finished block to the front of the bunting, again with running stitch. Here the block and front panel are both white, though contrasting colors could be used.

   Next, place the inside color of the bunting front on a table with the

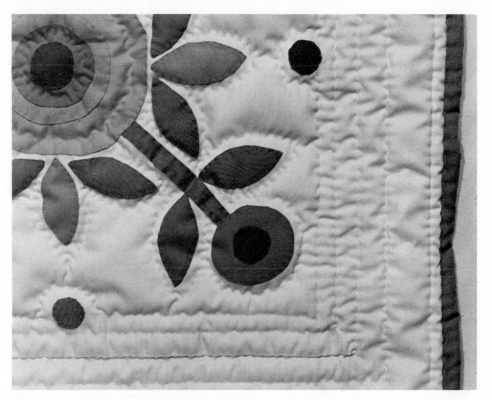

Detail—quilting stitches echo the appliqué design.

Appliqué pieces for the quilted bunting. (1 square = ½ inch)

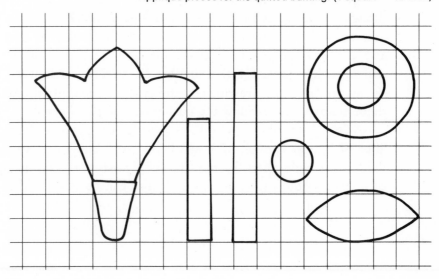

face side down. Put a layer of Dacron polyester batting over it, then place the bunting front, face side up, on top of that. Pin, then baste, the three layers together. Do the same for the bunting back.

Quilt the bunting front, letting the quilting stitches follow the shape of the appliqué and bunting. See page 181 on quilting for a more detailed description of the quilting process. Then quilt the bunting back, following the curve of the back arch. Bind the top edge of the bunting front.

Finally, place the quilted front on the quilted back, with bottom edges and sides matching. Pin and baste, then bind all the way around the outside. The binding here is cut from fabric which matches the inside color of the bunting.

This bunting is soft and fully padded so it easily replaces blankets when taking the baby out. It makes a good makeshift bed while visiting and eliminates the possibility of the baby kicking off his or her covers.

Yellow Bunting

The appliquéd soft yellow bunting is a lightweight version of the quilted bunting. The pattern for cutting the front and the back panels is the same. In this one, however, the back piece was not rounded into an arch but was left with square corners. Pale yellow is used for the inside, checkered gingham for the outside.

The design utilizes the same pattern pieces as the quilted bunting, though the parts are in a different arrangement. The two larger circles are not shown in the patterns. They are cut to finish at 11 inches (28 cm) and at 5¼ inches (13 cm). Use a plate for the larger circle pattern, and a bowl will probably serve for the smaller circle. Leaves, flowers, and smaller circles are from the drawings on the grid for the quilted bunting. Arrange them in any way or follow the pattern in the photograph.

When the appliqué is finished, arrange the parts of the bunting with a filler of cotton flannel, or a synthetic baby blanket. This will be much lighter in weight than the bunting filled with batting, and makes a good summer version. Either is washable and can be fluff-dried in the drier.

Lightweight summer bunting is quilted through
gingham, flannel, and backing fabric.

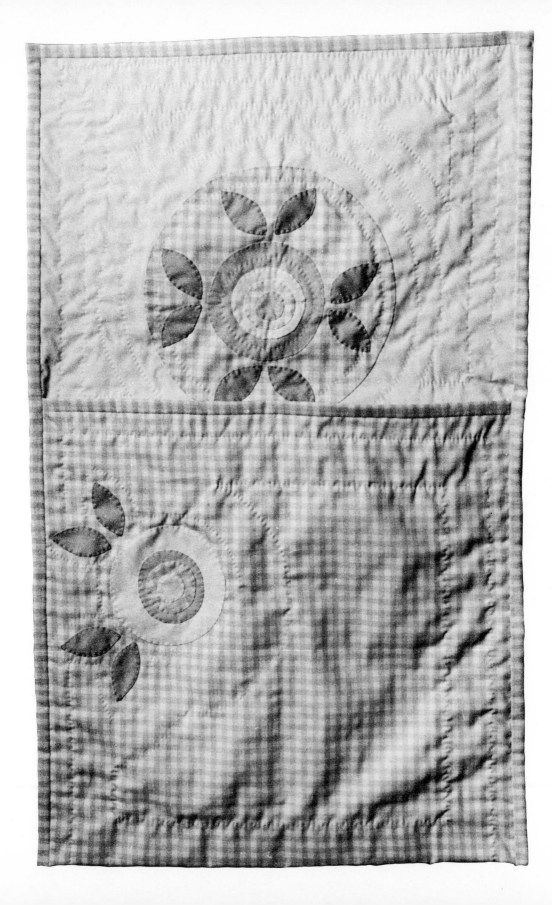

Wrap-up

Prequilted blue denim, lined with tiny checked blue gingham, offers a softly padded fabric for this handy wrap-up. It's great for car or travel and opens up to become a floor pad or nap pad when needed. Nina Stull added a berry design with machine appliqué, then used machine embroidery to add red leafy patterns. A few yellow French knots highlight the embroidery.

Cut the wrap-up according to the pattern. Do any decorative appliqué or embroidery next. Then fold the narrow top section, right sides together, and machine-stitch that seam to form the hood. Finish the seam on the inside. Then bind the

Winter wrap-up is prequilted denim by Nina Stull.

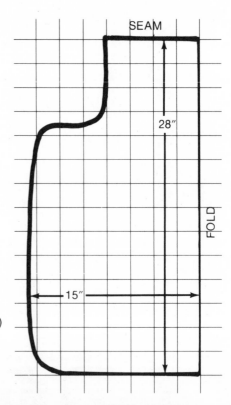

Pattern for wrap-up. (1 square = 2 inches)

entire wrap-up with a bias strip of contrasting color. Here a bright red bias was used to repeat the reds of appliqué and embroidery.

Velour Bunting

A sleeved bunting with zip-up front provides a snuggly wrap for winter. Bets Barnard used a beautiful velour for the bunting, then decorated it with rows and rows of edging. These include lines of chain stitching, white edgings, satin ribbons crisscrossed with gold threads, French knots, and laces. The finished effect is one of frosted splendor, fit for a prince or princess.

Make your patterns by the drawings on the grid. The bunting back is cut in one solid piece. The bunting hood is 16 inches (41 cm) long and 7 inches (43 cm) wide. Since the front has a zipper, fold additional material back.

All decorative work is added to the flat pieces of fabric. Then, always with the right sides of the fabric together, shoulder seams are joined. Add

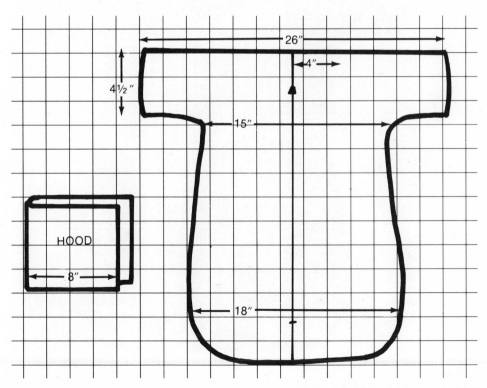

Velour bunting. (1 square = 2 inches)

the hood piece by placing the center of the strip in the center of the back and sewing it around the neckline to the front opening. Next the zipper is set into the front of the bunting. Sew the underarm and side seams. Finally the top of the hood is sewn together by joining it in a single seam down the top of the hood. Lining can be cut from the same pattern but with ½ of an inch (13 mm) less material at all outside edges. Slip it into the bunting and whipstitch the turned edges to the bunting.

Elegant velour bunting has white ribbons and trims with gold thread work.

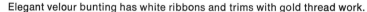

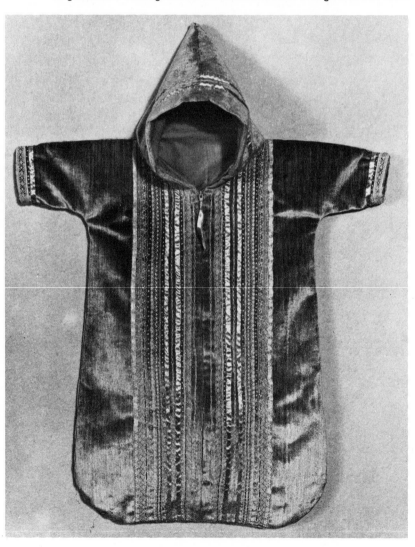

Fur-trimmed jacket has a matching bag to warm the toes.

Fur-trimmed Jacket and Bag

This orange velveteen outfit falls somewhere between a jacket and a sleeping bag. The pattern for the jacket on the grid is for a six-month-size. Use a printed lining that relates in color to the jacket. Add fur to the sleeves before sewing the arm seam. Do the same for the hood, so that ends of the fur trim will later be caught in the seams.

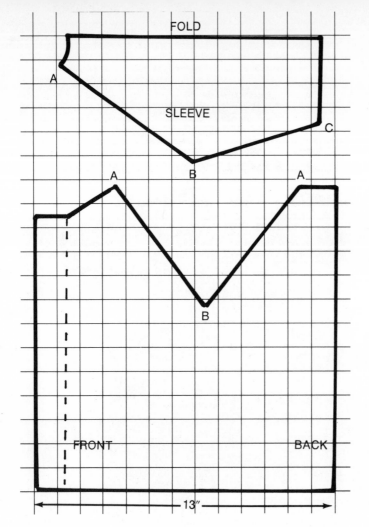

Fur-trimmed jacket pattern.
(1 square = 1 inch)

Sew sleeves to jacket by joining lines A–B of sleeve to A–B of jacket. Repeat for each side. Sew fur trim to ends of sleeves. Then sew sleeve seams, lines B–C, to form sleeves.

Cut lining the same as for the jacket except at dotted lines. Join the same way as for the jacket. Slip the lining inside the jacket. Fold the jacket material over lining at bottom edge of the jacket, the sleeves, and at the front of the jacket.

Join the hood by sewing line A–B to line A–C on each side. Line. Gather at back edge. Sew the front edge of hood material over raw edge of lining. Sew line to form channel and add fur trim.

Set hood on jacket, right sides together. Cut a 1-inch-wide (25-mm) bias binding to finish raw edge where hood and jacket are joined.

Pattern for fur-trimmed hood. (1 square = 1 inch)

143

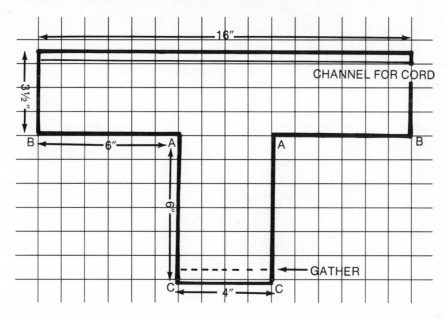

For the bag part, cut a rectangle 36 inches by 18 inches (92 cm by 46 cm) plus seam allowance. Fold in half crosswise to make a half sleeping bag. Sew side seams. Make a lining the same way, then fold the velveteen over the lining on the inside of the bag for a finished edge. Slip-stitch edges together. The jacket can be used separately, but the bag is helpful for trips in a car or to keep the napping baby warm.

Toddler's Sleeping Bag

Naptime turns into fun and games with a sleeping bag to crawl into. This one is made from prequilted fabric and is lined with checked gingham. A rectangle, cut 36 inches by 42 inches (92 cm by 107 cm) wide, provides the basic bag. Add any decorative work while the material is flat. To assemble, fold the fabric so that the two ends are brought together forming a shape 36 inches (92 cm) high and 21 inches (53 cm) wide. Stitch together from the bottom up to 10 inches (25 cm), then set in the zipper. In this bag a 16-inch (41-cm) zipper was used which left an opening flap at the top. With right sides facing, join a seam to make the foot of the bag. Be sure to keep the zipper at the center if you want a top-opening bag.

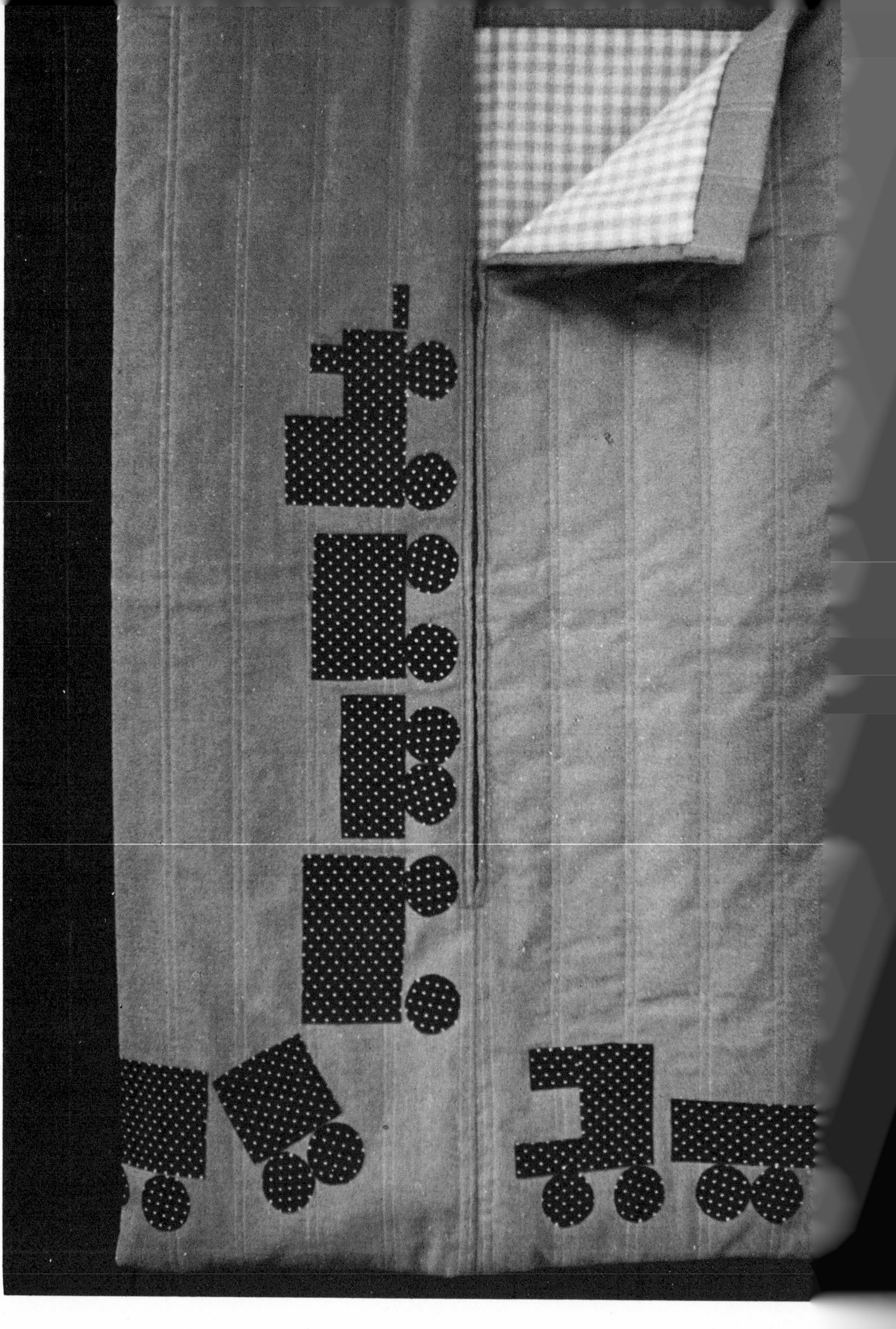

Sleeping bag for a toddler
zips down beside a polka-dot train.

145

To make a side-opening bag, just refold so that the zipper is at the side before you sew the bottom edges of the bag together.

Make a lining for the bag but cut it 2 inches (5 cm) shorter than the bag. Sew top of bag to top of lining, right sides of fabric together. Then sew the foot of the lining. Slip the lining in place inside the sleeping bag and slip-stitch edges next to the zipper and openings.

Add any decorative work before joining parts. The train was added to the flat material before any seams were taken and without the lining in place. Train shapes were cut by the patterns. Then identical shapes were cut from Stitch Witchery (or use any similar bonding material). Iron the designs in place, being sure to follow directions given for the adhesive material.

These same designs can be worked in machine appliqué, cut according to the drawings. To hand-appliqué, add a hem allowance to be turned under.

Toddler's sleeping bag decorations. (1 square = 1 inch)

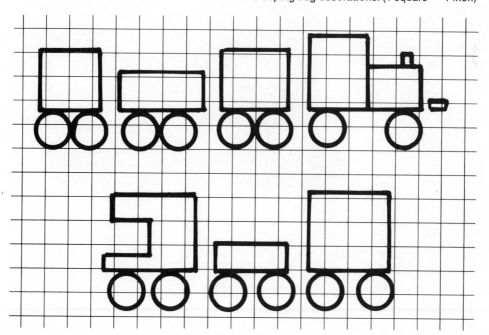

A train of iron-on tape puffs its way around this drawstring toy bag.

Train Toy Bag

Another train makes fun and games of picking up toys. This pillow-case-like bag is one piece of material folded over and sewn at side and bottom. Again all decorative work should be done first on the flat fabric. The train design is given in the drawing.

The bag was cut 36 inches long (92 cm) and about 3 inches (8 cm) was folded under at the top edge. A channel was sewn, 1 inch (25 mm) wide, to allow for a drawstring cord which closes the bag. The width of the fabric was folded in half to make a bag one-half as wide.

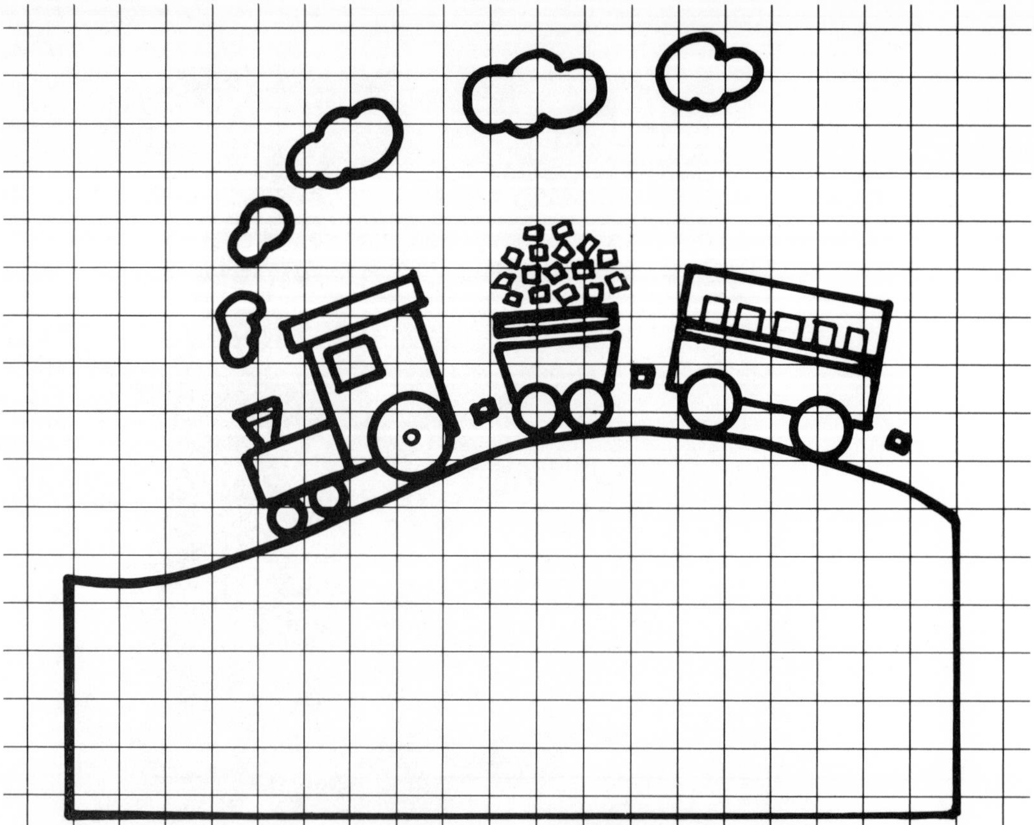

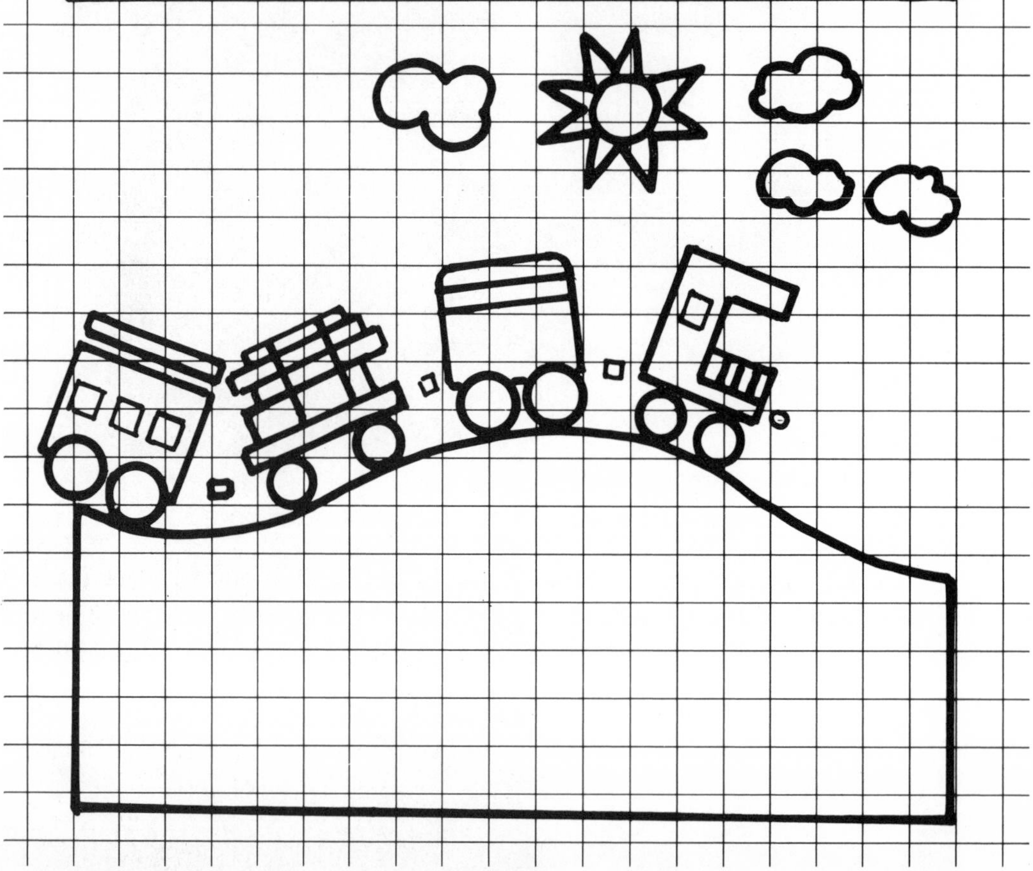

This train is cut from iron-on tape and applied directly, by ironing, to the bag. The hillsides over which the train runs can be appliquéd, or they can be applied by means of fabric adhesive. The iron-on patches in lightweight cotton are large enough for most of the train parts. On some of these, narrow strips of tape were used side by side to achieve a larger shape.

Flower Toy Bag

Felt appliqué designs, hand-sewn to a piece of upholstery fabric, make a colorful carryall or toy bag. Running stitches and French knots are sewn

An array of dazzling felt flowers brightens this toy or carryall bag of sturdy upholstery material.

150 in double strands of embroidery floss. The upholstery material of the bag is durable and sturdy, so it will withstand a lot of hauling and packing.

The front of the bag is 18 inches by 30 inches (46 cm by 76 cm), but an additional 4 inches (10 cm) is needed at the top to allow for turnover and drawstring closure. The back is cut to the same size. When the appliqué is finished, the top edges are hemmed. Then the front and back are joined at the sides and at the bottom.

The drawings, which are full scale, give a variety of designs to be used in an appliqué of this kind. To make a bouquet design similar to this, just add stems at the base and assemble a collection of flowers and leaves.

Flower toy bag

Sugar baby quilt. Rows of blanket-wrapped babies are lined up as they appear in the hospital nursery. Thirty-one inches by forty-two inches.

Sugar Baby Quilt

This delightful baby quilt was pieced of pink and white cotton fabrics. A minimum amount of appliqué and just a few lines of embroidery are added.

To make the quilt, cut the pieces A, B, C, and D as shown in the diagram. The details for the babies' faces are given in the full-scale draw-

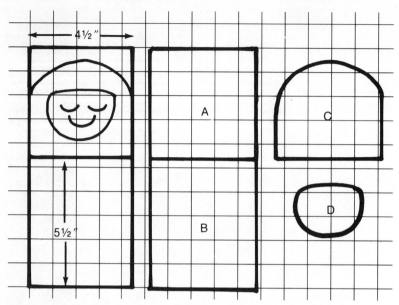

Diagrams for sugar baby quilt. (1 square = 1 inch)

Sugar baby's face—full scale

4½″ × 4½″

ing. Be sure to add seam allowances at each edge. Sew the arch shape C to block A, turning under the seam allowance on the curve and sewing with a running stitch. Leave bottom edge unsewn. Be sure to alternate colors, putting pink on white and white on pink. Then sew D to the top of C, as shown. Add embroidery, using an outline stitch with two strands of embroidery floss. Finish all the appliqué.

To make a quilt this size, which includes 28 sugar babies, cut as follows: A blocks: 16 pink, 12 white; B blocks: 16 white, 12 pink; C shapes: 16 white, 12 pink; D shapes: 16 pink, 12 white.

Then, to assemble the blocks, join block A to B, alternating colors. That is, on one block use a pink A and a white B. On the next use a white A and a pink B.

Now join the A–B blocks to one another, going across, to make a row of 7 sugar babies. Each row should start with a white B block and colors should alternate. Make a second row of 7 sugar babies, being sure that this row starts with the same color combination as the first row. Then join the two rows. Proceed this way until all the blocks are joined.

This design can be made up into a quilt of any size simply by adding more blocks. Use blue and white, if you prefer, for a boy. Or try some adventurous combinations.

To machine-appliqué this quilt, cut blocks A and B as shown, remembering to add seam allowance. Cut parts C and D with *no* seam allowance. Use a machine satin stitch at the outside edge of each.

When the quilt top is finished, join it to the backing and stuffing for quilting as described on page 179.

Biscuit Quilt

The puffy surface of this quilt is inviting and irresistibly attractive to young and old alike. It is made in the traditional biscuit or puff quilt method. The 6-inch (15-cm) squares of soft colored fabrics are tucked or gathered onto muslin backing pieces 3 inches (8 cm) square. The larger fabric square is placed, face side up, over the smaller one, with tucks or

Joining the biscuit quilt squares

Biscuit quilt is irresistible to a child looking for a place to nap.

gathers in place as in the drawing. It is machine-stitched on three sides, then stuffed, and the remaining fourth side is sewn shut.

Biscuits are stuffed with a polyester batting or with nylon stockings from which the thick areas at the top and the toe have been cut off. Then, with the puffy, right sides together, the blocks are sewn together in rows, and the rows are then joined. Add a backing and bind.

Betty Ferguson used 110 puffs in this quilt which is 10 puffs wide and 11 long or 32 inches by 36 inches. The edge is bound in a gingham which also appears in the blocks.

Nap Pad with Decorated Squares

This thickly padded and bright-colored nap pad can go from the bed to the floor, from the car to a picnic.

Blocks are cut to finish at 8 inches (20 cm) square. (These were cut 9 inches [23 cm] square, and ½-inch [13-mm] seams were taken at each side.) The 8 white squares were decorated with ball-point fabric markers and felt-tip marking pens. Alternating with these decorated pieces are squares of bright solid colors. They are joined together to make rows, then the rows are sewn together to make the completed top.

The top is assembled with a bonded quilt batt and a backing material as described on page 180. There are further directions on the use of the ball-point markers on page 186.

The pad is lined in a bright blue which also serves as the binding fabric. It is machine-quilted on the seam lines. A favorite drawing could be repeated in a variety of colors, rather than doing a separate drawing for each block.

Nap pad is machine-quilted on the seam lines. Twenty-six inches by forty-two inches.

Bright bold colors and childlike designs are combined in a simple block pattern.
Twenty-eight inches by thirty-seven inches.

8. *a gallery of ideas*

Here is a gallery of other ideas and projects. Many are personal and are not adaptable to patterns, but they are presented here to inspire you to designs of your own. Basic methods and structures are described to guide you in designing.

Wild Flower Quilt

This wildly colored quilt, made from Mexican cotton and kettle cloth, uses a whole variety of simple flower forms. Each one is on a 6-inch (15-cm) square of bright yellow, bordered in a riotous array of blues, reds, oranges, and greens.

Children's drawings can readily be adapted for appliqué of this kind. Blocks are hand-sewn and the assembled layers are hand-quilted.

Rainbow Mobile

Stuffed, round rolls of felt are joined to make the substantial rainbow in this mobile. A pot of gold drifts by at the end of the rainbow and blue birds sail endlessly above it.

158 The rainbow is 36 inches (91 cm) long, and the blue birds have a 12-inch (30 cm) wingspan. All parts of the mobile are stuffed with quilt batting and are hung from nylon leader (fish line) which virtually disappears in the air. They are suspended from a dowel.

A fat, sausage-like stuffed rainbow arches over a pot of gold in this mobile by Karen Jahncke.

The angel is part of a celestial mobile which includes clouds, stars, and a moon.
By Karen Jahncke.

Angel Mobile

Karen Jahncke's love of mobiles led her to produce this delightful collection of angels floating among the stars and a moon.

The angels are 20 inches from halo to toe. They are plump with batting and have embroidered features and curly yarn hair. Stars measure about 9 inches across.

All these stuffed celestial forms are suspended with nylon leader (fish line) from a wooden crosspiece. This allows the angelic cherubs to twist and turn in a never-ending orbit among the stars. Solid colors and prints are combined in the stuffed shapes. Hung above a crib or baby bed, the continuous gliding movements would lull any baby to sleep.

Elsie the Cow Quilt

Quilt designer, Doris Hoover, calls this "The Cows Are in the Nine Patch." She cut Elsie from a collection of Borden's Milk hand towels, then treated her to a series of spray and dye processes. The heads were then appliquéd with machine stitching to denim squares. Alternated with the denim blocks are other squares of prints, tie-dyes, and spray-dyed fabrics.

It is a marvelous variation on a theme with the Elsie blocks bordered in denim, then with prints and bright colors, and finally bound in denim. Hand quilting adds patterns at the borders.

Doris' quilt would delight not only the baby milk-consuming cham-

Detail shows how Elsie left her humdrum tea towel existence and found stardom, featured on these denim blocks.

Appliquéd flowers cover the front of this well-padded quilted bunting. (Photo by Gayle Smalley)

Fur-trimmed jacket has a matching half sleeping bag to keep legs wrapped and warm. (Photo by Stan Bitters)

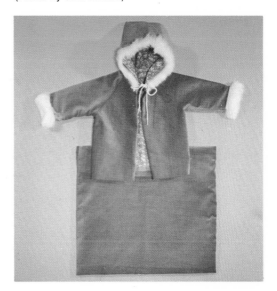

An iron-on train chugs all the way around this sleeping bag. (Photo by Stan Bitters)

Rainbow dress with bonnet by Wilanna Bristow combines polka-dotted pastels with a sky-blue background. (Photo by Stan Bitters)

Carryall bags are handy for travel and tuck in easily at the last minute. (Photo by Stan Bitters)

Appliqué and patchwork are combined with brilliant colors in this crib or carriage quilt. (Photo by Stan Bitters)

Doris Hoover's quilt features Elsie the Cow with spray and dye-treated fabrics.
Forty inches by fifty-two inches.

pion, but also any mother as well. Many ready-printed materials might be adapted to quilt-making in a similar way.

Chelsea's pillowcase was photo silk-screened on muslin, eighteen inches by twenty-eight inches. By Brian Wilhite and Ernie Smith.

Chelsea's Pillow

The baby's hospital identification picture was combined with illustrations from an old book to produce this print. The photo silk-screen process was used. This involves having a halftone print made on acetate, which can then be used to transfer the image to a photosensitive film on the silk screen. Anyone familiar with silk screening or with photographic processes will be able to manage this technique.

There are endless possible uses for these prints if you have access to the materials for making them. This print is on a pillowcase. It would be equally inviting on quilt blocks. Or even on a sweatshirt for the proud new father.

Three-Dimensional Family Tree

A full-blown family tree, designed by Nina Stull, has marvelous little felt figures to represent the interests and professions of various family members. The tree itself is built on a cord which runs through the center so it can be hung. The tree parts are made in graded sizes, starting with the smallest at the top. A 4-inch (10-cm) circle, cut into 6 wedges, gives

Three-dimensional family tree,
eighteen inches tall,
by Nina Stull.

the basic pattern for the first clump of leaves. Use that wedge as a pattern, add seam allowance, and cut 6. Join the 6 smaller ones to form the bottom half of the leaf clump. Join the top 6 (like putting together the slices of a pie) to make the dome shape for the top. Before joining top and bottom, machine-sew leaves to the top section. About 16 were used here. Join the two parts, stuffing as you go. Slip it onto the cord or string and hold it in place by knotting a bead onto the cord.

Repeat for the next two sections, using a 5-inch (13-cm) circle as pattern for the middle and a 6-inch (15-cm) circle on the bottom. Before sliding the middle sections onto the cord, sew two tree trunk pieces together, machine-stitch, and thread the cord through the middle. Repeat for the last section.

Finally, the objects are made to represent various family members. Some of those include a sewing machine for the designer herself and a globe for her geography-teacher husband. There could be blackboards for teachers, flasks for chemists, a mason jar for a home-canning enthusiast, and an ear of corn for a farmer. Each addition to the cord is knotted in place or secured with a bead.

The drawings suggest shapes similar to those used in the photographed tree.

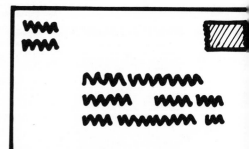

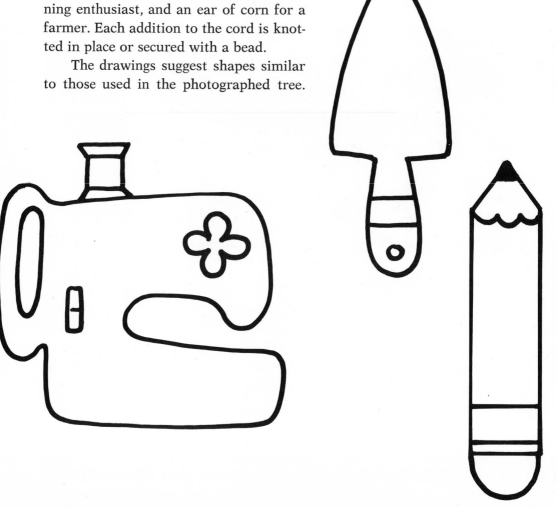

Rainbow Dress

Here is a beautiful dress, full of rainbows, to brighten a toddler's day. Use any simple dress pattern. Then add rolling hills and rainbows as stitchery designer Wilanna Bristow did. She used a green polka-dot hillside over the sky-blue dress. The rainbows are tiny polka dots in violet, pink, and yellow. The finished bands of the rainbows are about 1 inch wide. She sewed the top band of color first, then overlapped the second band on the first, the third band on the second. The size of the rainbows would vary according to the fullness of the skirt and size of the dress.

The pattern for the bird is given full size in the drawing. The bonnet

Wilanna Bristow designed this delicate pastel and sky-blue rainbow dress. The eyelet portion of the bonnet buttons onto the bonnet brim so that the wearer peers out from under the splendor of another rainbow.

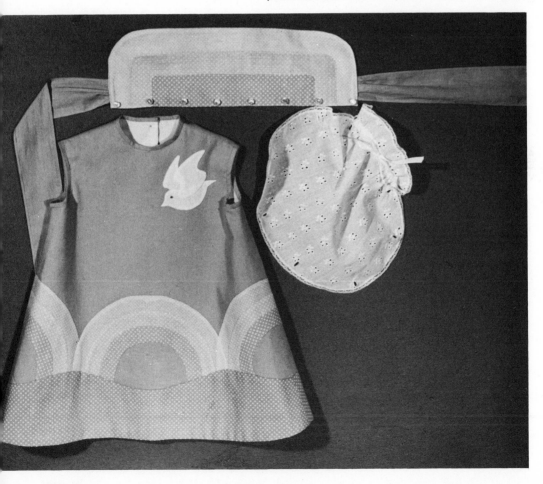

Bird motif for rainbow dress

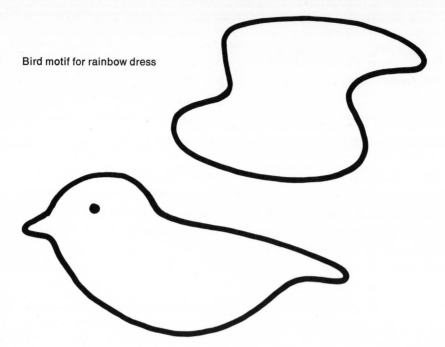

Bonnet and brim patterns for rainbow dress.
(1 square = 1 inch)

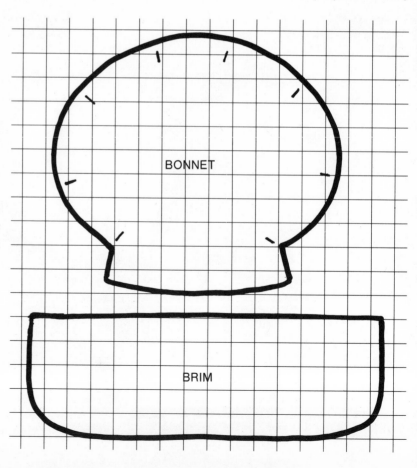

BONNET

BRIM

and brim patterns are on a grid. Buttonholes on the bonnet top match corresponding buttons sewn to the straight edge of the bonnet brim, which is also rainbow-striped. Cut it from a solid color first, then place the rainbow bands over the top.

Gown

An ordinary baby garment can be transformed into a distinctive gown through the addition of needlework. Here, cut-through appliqué and embroidery, all machine-sewn, make this a dazzling addition to any baby's wardrobe.

The gown pieces were cut double, one in white and one in red, and stacked red over white. As areas were cut out of the red, the white fabric showed through. Stitching is in red, deep red, and white.

Cut-through appliqué and embroidery were applied by Nina Stull to this colorful gown.

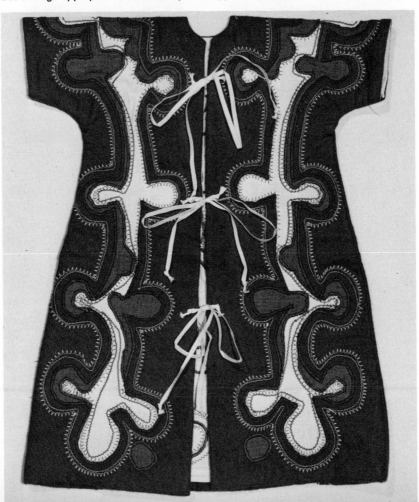

Raisin Dress

A small girl who *loves* raisins was given this dress by her mother. The raisin box was the source of the design, and the decorative label was translated to embroidery.

The bonnet and apron dress are of simple design and similar ones are available in commercial design patterns. Use any design which ap-

Raisin dress was sewn by Carol Zellmer for her daughter, patterned after the package of her favorite snack.

Detail of embroidery.

peals to you, and then let the child's own favorite flavors determine the design. Perhaps a passion for peanut butter or cocoa could provide a similar source of inspiration.

A small embroidered design on the back reads "Grown in California." The label has been changed, of course—the weight given is that of the little girl.

Cross-stitches form a red apple
on this checked gingham dress by Carol Zellmer.

Apple Dress

Another simple jumper is given special treatment with a cross-stitch design. Using gingham simplifies the whole thing, since the tiny checks of the fabric offer a grid pattern over which the stitches can be sewn.

The New Baby

This lovely panel by Shirli Adkins is adapted from an old family photograph. A printed fabric suggests a wallpaper pattern which serves as a backdrop for the mother and siblings of the newest arrival.

"The New Baby" is a nostalgic, lace-covered collage based on a family photo.
Sixteen inches by twenty-four inches.

The collage is made up of laces, fabrics, edgings, and prints, all carefully appliquéd. Some are padded to give them added dimension. Facial details are embroidered. The finished collage is mounted over a stiff board (such as illustration board) and then framed.

A stitchery tree supports hammock and sleeping baby doll on this nap pad by Lynette Hiebert.

Tree with a Hammock

The tree in this machine-appliquéd, padded panel is complete with raccoon, squirrel, and bird. It has a fabric hammock swinging in its branches. The doll, in her flannel nightie, can be lifted out of her tree-hung bed to be played with. This nap pad can be used on the floor or as a quilt.

The machine stitching was sewn through the top and the padding. The nap pad was then backed and bound in bright red.

Tablecloth Comforter

A lace tablecloth, sewn to a rich orange fabric, makes a beautifully patterned top for a comforter. Nylon tulle is layered over the lace to protect it. The comforter has a blanket for filler, and more of the bright orange for a backing fabric. The layers are tied together with yarns spaced over the entire comforter.

A tablecloth comforter shows orange fabric through the pattern of old lace. By Betty Ferguson.

"Transmogrification."
A formidable greeting by this glove man
reminds older brothers or sisters
that the baby is sleeping.
Six inches tall.
By Pat King.

"Transmogrification"

A stuffed glove, stitched and beaded, holds up a hand in absurdly sober greeting. The stuffing is packed into the glove before the stitching and beading are added. Stitching on the surface of the face shapes the features, and the beads add a fixed stare to an already serious look. When the decorative work is finished, a circle of cardboard is cut and set into the open end of the glove. It is covered with fabric and the base is slip-stitched shut.

This beaded handy man is fun to make, and if it's not fully appreciated by the new baby, it is *sure* to be enjoyed by the parents.

Of all gifts which can be made for the baby, it is undoubtedly those of personal or family significance which are most treasured. When you select specific ideas, whether it's the raisins in the raisin dress, a photograph of the new baby, or a name in a birth panel—then the gift takes on the special meaning which prompts someone to preserve it so that it can be enjoyed a second or even a third time around.

9. methods

Ways to use this book and detailed descriptions for quilting, binding, mounting, and lettering are in the following pages.

Using the Patterns in This Book

All patterns given in the drawings are for finished sizes: No seam allowances have been added. It is essential, when sewing woven fabric, that you add this allowance to each edge. The amount of allowance added is usually ⅜ of an inch (10 mm), but either ¼ or ½ of an inch (6 mm or 13 mm) can be used depending on your own sewing preference. The measurements for the patterns are in inches and no conversions to metric is given as the fractional differences in the metric conversion would alter the patterns.

When drawings or patterns are to be used for machine appliqué, do not add seam allowance. The satin stitch is sewn right on the raw edge and the material is not folded under.

When felt, or any other nonwoven and nonraveling material is used, do not add a seam allowance.

Some patterns are given full scale. Others, placed over a grid, are given on a scale of 1 square to 1 inch or 1 square to 2 inches. To enlarge these, draw a corresponding grid of intersecting lines (or use a large sheet of graph paper). If the small grid is 1 square to 2 inches, use a large grid in which lines are 2 inches apart. Then copy the drawing from the small grid to the large.

Many other drawings are scattered throughout this book to offer ideas for all kinds of needlework. They can be used as design sources or they can be enlarged and used as patterns.

Choice of Fabrics and Materials

Careful consideration must be given to the selection of materials used in toys, clothes, or blankets for babies. Each fabric has certain advantages as well as drawbacks, and sometimes these must be balanced against one another in choosing.

Synthetic fabrics, nonallergenic materials, and washable battings are a boon, but may not be the best solutions in all situations. Cotton fibers, like any of the natural fibers, are absorbent. They are cooler in summer and more comfortable to wear. Synthetics wash and dry easily and many require no ironing. Always read fiber contents of materials purchased and make a note of any special washing or cleaning instructions.

Cotton flannel, because of problems with flammability, has recently been under careful scrutiny. This material is now identified in terms of its suitability for children's clothes. Check labels for this information. Synthetic flannels are now available which have a similar softness.

Since various kinds of fabric finishes are now used, it is always advisable to wash any material before it comes in contact with the baby's skin. While most finishes are harmless, occasional allergies and reactions do occur.

Any hard objects, such as buttons or beads, must be securely attached if they are to be used on baby's playthings or clothes. Sew firmly with strong threads and then resew. When babies are at a mouthing stage (where things are "felt" by being placed in the mouth), avoid fur, yarn tassels, hanging bells, or similar inappropriate objects. If certain toys are for visual pleasure but not for handling, be sure that they are kept out of reach.

Any fabric that has been hand-painted, dyed, or decorated with felt or ball-point markers must be washed to remove any excess dye or coloring agent.

"Sugar Babies," a pieced and appliquéd cradle quilt.

Assembling a Quilt

A quilt consists of three layers of material which are assembled and held together with quilting stitches. Usually the three layers include the *decorative top*, the *filler*, and the *backing*.

The *decorative top* may be pieced, appliquéd, or made up of a combination of the two. Pieced quilts (those in which small geometric pieces of fabric are joined together to make the pieced top) are usually of cotton or cotton/synthetic fabrics. Heavier fabrics, like cotton velveteen, work well where a single length of fabric makes the background. Velveteens are somewhat bulky or heavy if very small pieces of fabric are required.

Appliqué is most easily done with cotton fabric if it is to be handsewn. For machine appliqué, heavier materials such as denims and velveteen may be used.

Fillers for quilts consist generally of either of two kinds of materials: batting or woven fabric. Batting is now usually Dacron or polyester, and comes in a loose batt or a glazed batt. The loose batt unrolls to make more or less of a sheet. It can be peeled into thinner layers. It is this batt which can be plucked apart for stuffing dolls or animals. I prefer it for all hand quilting. The glazed batt has a somewhat hard, smooth surface and its primary advantage is that it will not come apart or shift when it is washed. If a quilt is to have a minimum of quilting stitches, or must be especially durable (as for a floor pad or crawl pad), the glazed batt is preferable.

When batting seems to be too thick, too heavy, or too warm for your purposes, a woven material may be used as filler. Cotton flannel is one of the most common. Flannel must be preshrunk if it is purchased as yardage. Some flannel-like baby blankets are actually made of synthetics and will not shrink. Any preshrunk blanket can be used as filler. I have sometimes used a sheet of muslin or broadcloth when I wanted only the thinnest filler. The real advantage to the woven filler is that quilting can be widely spaced, since nothing will shift. In fact, woven fillers may be used to add padding where there is to be no quilting at all.

The *backing* fabric is the material which shows on the reverse side of a quilt. A print is often used, since there is no decorative work on the back. It should be a lightweight material that is easy to sew through.

To prepare any pieced or appliquéd material for assembly and quilting, the fabrics should be pressed smooth. The backing fabric is placed right side down on a large smooth surface (a big table or the floor). The filler is placed over the backing. Most beginning quilters tend to use too much batting rather than too little. Both backing and filler should be the same size or larger than the quilt top—never smaller. The quilt top is placed face side up over the backing and filler as in the drawing. All layers are pinned together, then basted. Usually basting lines run up and down, across, and diagonally. For a large quilt, a grid pattern of basting lines about 6 inches apart is needed, as shown.

Positioning the quilt top

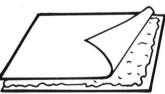

Grid pattern for quilt's basting lines

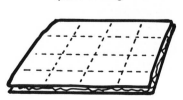

All the hand-quilted articles shown in this book were quilted without a quilting frame. If you are more comfortable or at home with a quilting frame, by all means use one. But it is not essential. My experience suggests that it is much easier to work without a frame.

Once the basting is completed, the quilt should be turned over to check for wrinkles or folds. If any wrinkles have occurred, that line of basting must be taken out and resewn so that the fabric is smooth. When the back of the quilt is smooth, with no folds in the basting, quilting may begin.

Next you need to decide if you are going to quilt by hand or by machine. Examples in this book show both methods.

Hand Quilting

Use quilting thread or heavy-duty thread in a color that is dominant in the quilt top. If you are new to quilting and don't want stitches to show too much, use a matching thread. If quilting is where you shine, use a contrasting color. Use quilting thread single, knotting one end and leaving the other end free.

Hand quilting is easiest if it goes in straight lines. For example, to make a pattern around blocks, quilt straight lines which cross, as shown in the drawing. You get the same effect, but it's easier to sew and looks neater. If you sew within each square, the stitches tend to gather slightly and round out the corners.

Straight lines of quilting
outline quilt blocks

As you quilt, check the quilt back to make sure no wrinkles appear. Pull stitches tight enough to texture the layers of material, but don't pull *too* tight or there will be excess tension on the thread. Hide knots at the beginnings of rows, or in seam lines. Finish a thread by taking an extra overcast stitch on the back and then reversing the direction for two or three stitches, hiding them in the thickness of the quilt.

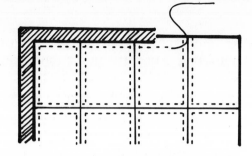

The last line of quilting sewn
after the quilt is bound

When quilting around blocks, leave the outside line of quilting until later. After the binding is added and finished, the last line of quilting stitches can be sewn as shown in the drawing. This makes it easier to keep those two lines parallel and neat.

Machine Quilting

Machine quilting can be used on a number of these projects. While there is a great variety of possible methods in machine quilting, all of these examples use the same one. In it the quilted line is sewn exactly on a seam line. This causes the material to puff up, to appear very full, but hides the stitching.

The glazed batt or woven filler are recommended for machine quilting. If the batting is too thick, the machine may balk, or refuse to sew altogether. The thinner the layers of the quilt, the more easily it can be sewn.

The basting must be done as carefully as for hand quilting. Always sew lines of quilting in the same direction; that is, if the first line goes from the right side to the left, all those lines should start at the right side and go to the left. To alternate directions sometimes makes the fabrics pucker. When quilting is completed, the raw edges of the fabrics are ready for binding.

Binding

Binding is a means of finishing the raw edges of a quilt or panel by using strips of fabric. The width of the binding strip determines the width of the border.

Binding strips should be cut an inch or two longer than the edges they are to bind. With the panel or quilt right side up, place a binding

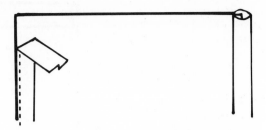

Trim edges of binding even with quilt or panel

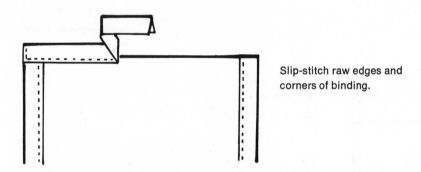

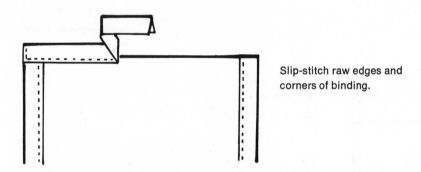

strip at one raw edge, with edges together and right sides of the fabric facing each other. Baste or pin, then machine-stitch exactly on the seam line. Trim ends of binding even with quilt or panel.

Next, do the opposite edge, so that either both sides or both top and bottom are sewn first. Fold the bindings over the raw edges and slip-stitch in place on the back side.

Next, do the remaining two edges. Place binding strips over the raw edges and out past the finished sections of binding. Baste or pin and sew. Turn binding and slip-stitch on reverse side. Trim to within ¼ inch (6 mm) of outside edge—do *not* cut binding even with the raw edge as you did on the first two strips. This allowance must be turned under to make a finished corner. Slip-stitch raw edges, then corners as in the drawing.

Slip-stitch raw edges and corners of binding.

To make a stuffed binding, which is sometimes desirable on a quilt, sew the edge of the binding in place as described. Before slip-stitching the open edge to the back side, add extra batting in the fold of the binding, to give it a full, stuffed look. Then slip-stitch. Repeat for the other strips of binding.

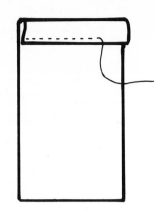

Panels and Wall Hangings

A simple way of finishing a wall hanging is to make a wide hem at the top through which a rod can be inserted. If you use felt, the edge can be turned back and no other hemming or finishing is required.

Use a running stitch to hold the hem in place. Baste first, then sew it from the face side so that stitches will appear even. If there is not enough material available at the top to hem as is shown in the drawing, add a strip of felt, cloth, or grosgrain ribbon and sew as shown.

To line a panel, select a lightweight fabric and press the seam allowance at the sides and at the bottom of the lining. Then place the lining over the hemmed panel. Turn edges under and slip-stitch lining to panel as in the drawing.

Stitching the hem in place

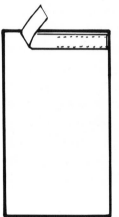

Slip-stitching lining to panel

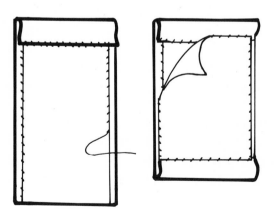

Mounting Panels

Mounting a fabric means to affix it more permanently to a board. Plywood is commonly used for the board, since it is available in any width. Plywood ½ of an inch (13 mm) thick is sufficient for large pieces, and ¼ of an inch (6 mm) will do for small pieces.

To mount a felt panel on plywood, lay the felt piece over the cut piece of plywood to determine correct placement. Pin or mark the edges. Then coat the flat surface of the wood with white glue. When it is somewhat set but not dry (a few minutes), place the felt on the wood according to the marks. Press with your hands to smooth it. When dry, the edges of the board can be glued and the excess felt at the corners clipped away. Extra felt at the sides or top and bottom is pulled to the back and glued or stapled.

To mount regular woven fabric to wood, place the material over the plywood to be sure the placement is accurate. A minimum of about 2 inches of fabric is needed at each of the four sides to mount fabric this way. No glue is used when mounting lightweight fabric. Pin or baste the fabric to mark the outline where it covers the surface of the plywood. Then place the fabric, face side down, on a tabletop. Put the plywood over the top, lining it up with the pins or basting marks. (Be sure the pins are on the face side.) Then draw the outside edges of the fabric around the back of the plywood. Staple in place. Fold or miter the corners so that extra material is evenly distributed. Staple evenly on all four sides. Cover the back side with a piece of felt or fabric slip-stitched to the stapled fabric.

The mounted panel can be hung this way or it can have a wood frame added.

Pillows

A pillow consists of two basic parts—the *pillow form* and the *pillow cover*. The *pillow form* is the muslin fabric filled with Dacron, kapok, or other filling material. When these are purchased, a finished size is usually given. For example, you can purchase a 14-inch pillow form at a needlecraft shop. That means that it measures 14 inches from seam to seam. It will fit a pillow cover that finishes at 14 inches square. If the pillow form is an inch larger than the pillow cover, it can be eased in and the excess size will just plump up into the pillow. If the pillow form is *smaller* than the pillow cover, there will always be excess fullness in the covering fabric.

The *pillow cover* which slips over the pillow form consists of a pillow top and a backing. The pillow top is the area to which decorative work is usually added. When a pillow top is completed, a pillow backing is cut to exactly the same size. Then the two are placed with right sides facing and are machine-stitched. All four corners should be machine-sewn, as in the drawing. That avoids the difficulty of hand-sewing a corner. Excess fabric is clipped off at the corners.

Machine-sewn corners for pillow cover

The unsewn space is for turning the pillow cover right side out and for inserting the pillow form. Then the opening is slip-stitched shut.

Fabric Markers

Various markers have been designed specifically for fabric and for permanence. They are of two general types—felt markers and ball-point markers. They are sometimes called fabric markers or fabric pens.

Felt markers are available in tips varying in size from a fine line to a very wide flat tip. Some are permanent and some are not, so it is important to test-wash markers on the fabric before launching into a full-scale project. Laundry markers, usually in black, are permanent, but the permanence often varies with the fiber contents of the material. *Be sure to read labels.* Some markers have a petroleum distillate base and pro-longed breathing of the vapors may be harmful. This information is printed on the label and precautions should be observed. If children are using the markers, special care must be taken. Working outdoors may be helpful as good ventilation is essential. Most felt-tip markers are inks or dyes and will be affected by the color of the fabric on which they are used.

Ball-point markers made especially for fabric (such as Vogart and Liquid Embroidery) come in a good variety of colors and are permanent. Again, it is important to test them on the fabric you intend to use. These colors are more opaque, leaving a layer of coloring material on the surface.

Ball-point fabric markers combined with marking pens to create the brightly colored design in this detail from Nina Stull's nap pad.

Needlepoint markers may also be used on fabric. Again be sure to read labels and observe precautions, as they vary in washability and brilliance. It is sometimes helpful to stretch fabric over a cardboard or to keep it taut in an embroidery hoop. A solid base is needed underneath to press the markers against.

India ink is permanent on fabric and may therefore be used to write or draw on various projects. It can be applied by brush, pen, or with the rubber-stamp letters of a child's printing set. To use a printing set, the letters can be pressed onto a gauze pad wet with India ink. The regular stamp-pad ink, usually in blue or black, will be satisfactory on anything that doesn't have to be washed. Try printing on scraps of fabric to determine which fibers accept the ink best. Cotton is usually good, especially a somewhat heavy absorbent weave.

Lettering

To simplify the cutting of lettering for felt appliqué, use these guidelines. First determine how high you want the letters to be. Those in the name panels of chapter 1 are about 1½ inches.

Cut a strip of fabric to the desired width. Start with 1¼ inches to 1½ inches and try that first. See the drawing. The top and bottom of each letter is now cut, so the lettering is half finished.

Next, cut sections off that strip for your letters, guessing as to the width of each. Most will be approximately square. See the drawing. An *i*

Beginning felt lettering strips

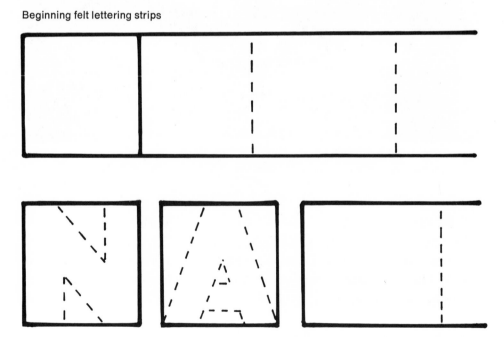

The lettering for this name panel was cut from felt and appliquéd.

will be narrow, a *w* will be wide. As soon as you cut these sections, the letters are nearly complete—just a few jogs to finish them off.

Remember that in felt appliqué the lines should be full, making fat letters. They are visually more appealing than skinny letters. Remember, too, that since your letters are identical in color and in height, some variation in the widths of the individual letters will not matter.

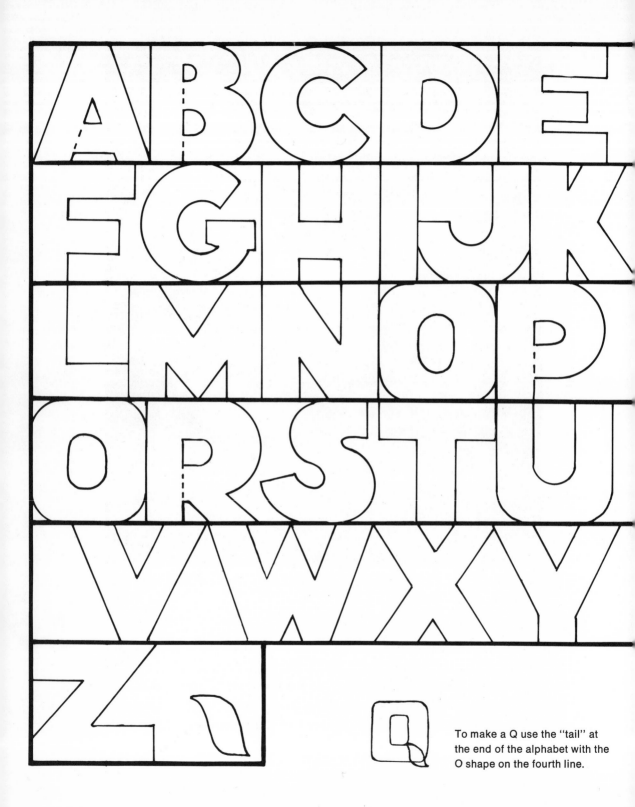

To make a Q use the "tail" at the end of the alphabet with the O shape on the fourth line.

The drawing shows a simple alphabet cut in this manner. The dotted lines indicate where scissors cuts are made right into the letter. For example, on the letter *A* it is very difficult to cut out the tiny triangle, so cut in from one edge. This makes enough room to handle the scissors in clipping out the triangle. When the letters are sewn, these cut edges are eased back together.

Standard Sizes

If you are planning to make quilts, sheets, or pillowcases, here are some standard measurements to guide you. These need not be rigidly adhered to. Obviously a quilt can be used, regardless of its dimensions, in one way or another. If you are making a nap pad, and want it to fit in the playpen or crib, then these figures will be helpful. Most quilts and sheets need a minimum of 3 inches to 6 inches to tuck in.

Crib mattress size: 27 inches or 28 inches by 52 inches
Crib sheet: 36 inches by 45 inches
Small crib sheet: 27 inches by 36 inches
Bassinet sheet: 18 inches by 27 inches
Baby pillow: 12 inches by 16 inches (many are smaller)
Pad for basket or bassinet: 13 inches by 28 inches
Playpen pad: 38 inches by 38 inches, 40 inches by 40 inches,
    or 39 inches by 44 inches